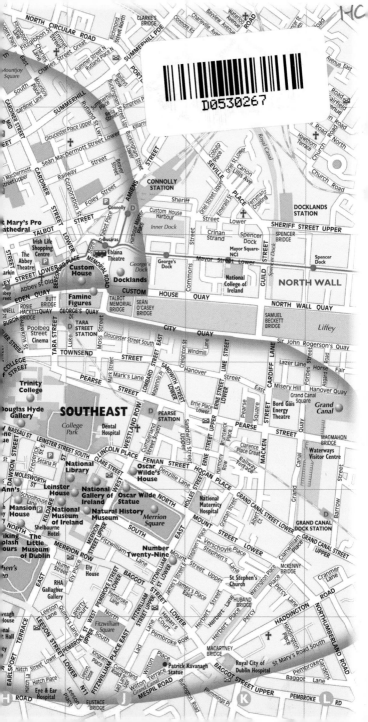

CITYPACK GUIDE TO
Dublin

How to Use
This Book

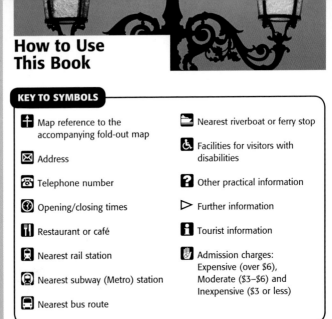

This guide is divided into four sections

• **Essential Dublin:** An introduction to the city and tips on making the most of your stay.

• **Dublin by Area:** We've broken the city into four areas, and recommended the best sights, shops, entertainment venues, nightlife and restaurants in each one. Suggested walks help you to explore on foot.

• **Where to Stay:** The best hotels, whether you're looking for luxury, budget or something in-between.

• **Need to Know:** The info you need to make your trip run smoothly, including getting about by public transportation, weather tips, emergency phone numbers and useful websites.

Navigation In the Dublin by Area chapter, we've given each area of the city its own color, which is also used on the locator maps throughout the book and the map on the inside front cover.

Maps The fold-out map accompanying this book is a comprehensive street plan of Dublin. The grid on this fold-out map is the same as the grid on the locator maps within the book. We've given grid references within the book for each sight and listing.

Contents

Introducing Dublin

Although the Celtic Tiger, as the Irish economy was nicknamed in the 1990s, has now been tamed and the buoyant mood has tempered, building and renovation in Dublin continues apace. The culture remains buzzing, youthful and cosmopolitan.

With the economic boom came an influx of artists, musicians, film-makers, chefs and designers attracted by tax concessions and inexpensive property. Its roaring success made it one of the most expensive countries in Europe. Then came the world recession. A downturn in the economy saw sky-high property values plummet and jobs disappear. The sleek and speedy Luas light rail system and the Port Tunnel are two legacies of the high-spending years that have made travel in and around the city much easier, and the spectacular Samuel Beckett Bridge has given Dublin a new landmark.

To the visitor, there are few signs of economic troubles. There's a buzz in the streets and the stylish restaurants and cafés; pubs and smart bars always seem busy. Shopping is as good as ever, and sales make the merchandise, from designer fashion to traditional and modern crafts, even more tempting. Dublin's cultural scene thrives, with theater productions, concerts and big stars performing at music venues, including the state-of-the-art 14,000-seater O2 arena. Traditional Irish music drifts from pubs, and DJs keep clubs hopping into the early hours.

If some building has stopped, much has continued. The innovative modern architecture of the rejuvenated Docklands has opened up exciting new urban spaces, and there's more to come. But the old city is still there, its Georgian buildings and squares never ceasing to delight. Museums and art galleries are packed with well-displayed treasures, there's history at every turn, and the people are as friendly and welcoming as their legendary charm suggests. A visit to Dublin is a great experience.

Facts + Figures

THE SPIRE OF DUBLIN
● At 120m (394ft), the O'Connell Street sculpture is one of the world's largest.
● Constructed from reflective stainless steel, the top 12m (39ft) are illuminated.
● Its official name is Monument of Light. Dubliners have still to learn to love it.

CRAIC

Craic (pronounced 'crack') is a word that describes fun, laughter and an overall good time. In Ireland people, places and events can all be 'great *craic*'. Pubs are the place for the *craic*, not just for drinking; they are where people join together for music, singing and talking. Dublin is very much a café society, but the pub remains at the heart of its social life.

NICKNAMES

It is a tradition in Dublin to have nicknames for the numerous statues and monuments dotted around the city. For example, spot the following:

● The Flue with the View
● The Hags with the Bags
● The Tart with the Cart
● The Stiletto in the Ghetto
● The Crank on the Bank
● The Quare in the Square

FASHIONABLE DISTRICT

Dignitaries and celebrities often stay slightly outside central Dublin, on the southeast side of the city. The fashionable area of Ballsbridge and Lansdowne Road is near the Aviva Stadium, hosting international rugby and football, the Royal Dublin Society's arena and the exclusive embassy belt with its excellent restaurants and classy hotels.

A Short Stay in Dublin

DAY 1

Morning It wouldn't be a true trip to Ireland without acquainting yourself with the 'black stuff' and an early start at the **Guinness Storehouse** (▷ 30–31) will help you beat the crowds. You can get a bus down to St. James's Gate and spend a couple of hours touring the displays.

Mid-morning Take your free glass of Guinness and maybe a coffee at the Gravity Bar at the top of the Storehouse and you will be rewarded with some of the best views of the city. Catch a bus or walk back to view **Christ Church Cathedral** (▷ 26), and a trip around the adjoining **Dublinia** (▷ 27) will give you an excellent insight into the medieval life of the city.

Lunch Walk from the cathedral down Lord Edward Street into Dame Street. Just opposite **Dublin Castle** (▷ 28–29) you will find a quaint tea shop, the **Queen of Tarts** (▷ 44), where you can get an excellent light lunch. After lunch you may wish to visit the castle and the **Chester Beatty Library** (▷ 25), a rare and priceless book and Oriental art collection.

Afternoon Continue to the bottom of Dame Street, taking a left turn into Anglesea Street. Carry on until you come to the quay, and take a left and go first right over the Ha'Penny Bridge for good views of the River Liffey. Over the river cross two roads and you will come to the **shopping malls** (▷ 57) of Abbey Street and Henry Street. To the right you can follow through to **O'Connell Street** (▷ 52–53).

Dinner Return over the Ha'Penny Bridge and go straight into **Temple Bar** (▷ 34) with its choice of cosmopolitan restaurants, bars and pubs.

Evening Soak up the atmosphere of Temple Bar and take in a traditional Irish music session at **Oliver St. John Gogarty** (▷ 40).

DAY 2

Morning *The Book of Kells* in Trinity College (▷ 72–73) is one of the most visited sights in Dublin and it is best to view as early as you can; the library opens at 9.30am.

Mid-morning Walk round the front of the college and into Dublin's premier shopping street, Grafton Street, with its high street names and designer shops. Stop for a coffee at the famous **Bewley's Café** (▷ 85). At the bottom of Grafton Street you will come to the **St. Stephen's Green Centre** (▷ 81), with **St. Stephen's Green** (▷ 70–71) to the left.

Lunch If the weather is nice have a picnic in the park—where you might be lucky enough to catch a concert in summer—or grab a bite to eat at the mall; try **Wagamama** (▷ 88) for something different.

Afternoon Take a stroll round the green, then take the exit to the north and cross over to Kildare Street. This is where you will find the grandest buildings in the city and fine museums, including the **National Museum** (▷ 66–67). Continue round to **Merrion Square** (▷ 75) with its wonderful reclining statue of **Oscar Wilde** (▷ 76). Wilde lived in the house opposite (▷ 76), on the corner of Merrion Square.

Dinner This is the locality of many of Dublin's top restaurants. Treat yourself at **Restaurant Patrick Guilbaud** (▷ 88) in the **Merrion Hotel** (▷ 112) on Upper Merrion Street or the Michelin-starred **L'Ecrivain** (▷ 86) in Lower Baggot Street, but expect to pay a price.

Evening You can choose here from traditional pubs or smooth, classy bars—the city is at your feet.

Top 25

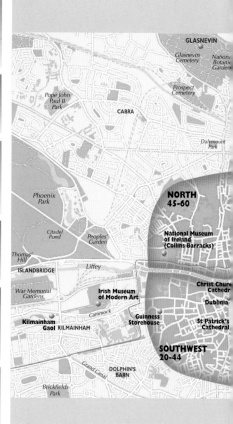

ESSENTIAL DUBLIN TOP 25

▶ ▶ ▶

Bank of Ireland ▷ 24
One of Dublin's grandest and most impressive
Palladian buildings.

Casino, Marino ▷ 92
A captivating 18th-century
villa set in the suburb
of Marino.

Chester Beatty Library
▷ 25 A most impressive
library of Oriental and
religious objects.

Trinity College ▷ 72–73
Ireland's premier seat of
learning houses perhaps
the most beautiful book in
the world.

Temple Bar ▷ 34 With
its bohemian reputation
and buzzing nightlife you
won't get a quiet pint here.

St. Stephen's Green
▷ 70–71 Take a quiet
break in this pleasant
green space in the heart of
Georgian Dublin.

St. Patrick's Cathedral
▷ 33 An embodiment of
the history and heritage of
the Irish people.

O'Connell Street
▷ 52–53 The revamped
thoroughfare reflects
poignant moments in the
city's history.

Number Twenty Nine
▷ 69 A gem of Georgian
architecture displaying
typical 18th-century middle-
class life.

**Natural History
Museum** ▷ 68 Step back
in time to view stuffed
animals and skeletons.

National Museum
▷ 66–67 This is the place
to come to see some great
national treasures.

National Gallery ▷ 65
Ireland's foremost collection
of art pays homage to the
old masters.

8

These pages are a quick guide to the Top 25, which are described in more detail later. Here they are listed alphabetically, and the tinted background shows the area they are in.

Christ Church Cathedral
▷ **26** The seat of Irish bishops since the time of Viking Dublin.

Collins Barracks ▷ **48**
An impressive building housing a dazzling national art collection.

Dublin Castle ▷ **28–29**
The hub of historic Dublin and seat and symbol of secular power.

Dublin City Gallery The Hugh Lane ▷ **49** Gallery of Irish artists among a host of well-known painters.

Dublin Writers Museum
▷ **50** A glowing tribute to the great literary figures of the city.

Dublinia ▷ **27** Relive life in Viking and medieval Dublin with this state-of-the art exhibition.

Glasnevin ▷ **93** Botanic Gardens and a graveyard that's a Who's Who of modern Ireland.

Grand Canal ▷ **64**
Part of the ambitious city regeneration project.

Guinness Storehouse
▷ **30–31** Celebrating 250 years of the 'black stuff' in a high-tech modern museum.

Irish Museum of Modern Art ▷ **96** Internationally acclaimed artists sit alongside local names.

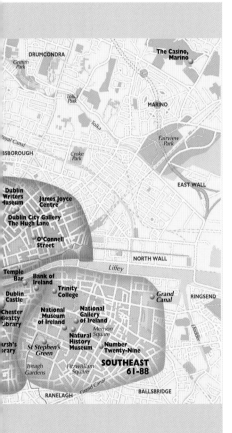

Marsh's Library ▷ **32**
An impressive collection is housed in Ireland's first public library.

Kilmainham Gaol
▷ **94–95** An atmospheric insight into profound moments of Irish history.

James Joyce Centre
▷ **51** This cultural attraction is devoted to the great man of Irish literature.

◀ ◀ ◀

Shopping

The delight of shopping in bustling Dublin lies in the compact nature of the city and the proximity of the best shopping areas to one another. Top designers and major fashion brands are represented, as are traditional stores and retro shops.

Variety Is the Key

What really makes shopping in Dublin rewarding is the variety and mix of shops to be found there. Small specialist shops tuck in alongside familiar high street names, and home-grown talent blossoms amid international brands. Craftspeople merge the traditional with the modern while they continue to work in wood, silver, glass, ceramics, linen and wool–their designs stylishly up to the minute. In Dublin you can find the best in beautifully made items, trendy home interiors and top-quality Irish food products.

Shopping Areas

Grafton Street, located south of the river, has always been considered the smart shopping area of the city. With its street musicians and colorful flower stalls, there's always a buzz in this pedestrian street lined with international and Irish fashion designer shops and chain stores, with the iconic Bewley's an essential coffee-stop along the way. Nearby, the Powerscourt Centre is the antidote to modern shopping malls. This fine 18th-century Georgian mansion plays host to more than 40 specialty boutiques and relaxing restaurants, bars and cafés. It's a calm

Brown's store (top); fashionable Grafton Street (middle); Crown Alley, Temple Bar (bottom)

KNOW YOUR *BODHRÁN* FROM YOUR BANJO

The *bodhrán* (pronounced 'bough-rawn') is a simple and very old type of frame drum made of wood with animal skin–usually goat–stretched over the frame and beautifully decorated. It is played with a double-ended stick, unlike most others which are struck with the hands. Played for centuries in Ireland, it came on to the world stage in the 1960s with the rise of the Irish band The Chieftains. If you can't master the technique, try hanging it on your wall!

and pleasing place to search for treasure. The Trinity College end of Grafton Street, Suffolk Street and Nassau Street are famed for their Irish design shops. The major department stores and big, bright and airy shopping centers are north of the river on O'Connell Street and Henry Street. With good parking, this revitalized area rivals Grafton Street for the attention of Dublin shoppers.

Irish Products

Sample bohemian South Great George's Street, filled with second-hand, retro and ethnic stores. Explore Temple Bar's cobbled winding streets for off-beat finds and Saturday markets. Francis Street is Dublin's antiques quarter, home to wonderful Irish furniture and silver. Shop for Aran knitwear—every sweater is unique—and Donegal tweed, Waterford, Tipperary and Galway crystal, Mosse pottery, Belleek porcelain, Orla Kiely bags and fine Irish linen. Jewelry has a special place in Dublin; look for the exquisite replicas of the Tara Brooch, Claddagh rings and Celtic knots mixing modern design with tradition, and the work of new young designers with creative flair, especially around Cow's Lane and the outdoor Designer Mart held there on Saturdays. In home interior shops you'll find contemporary designs based on time-honored patterns. Dublin is the place to buy traditional musical instruments. And although much is mass-produced in the Far East, kitsch is still part of Irish culture. To be sure, leprechauns, shamrocks and shillelaghs can be found in profusion.

Temple Bar (top); Penny's store in Mary Street (middle); St. Stephen's Green mall (bottom)

LOCAL DELICACIES

Breads, farmhouse cheeses and salmon are a few of the local delights, along with handmade fresh cream chocolates and truffles. The Saturday market in Meeting House Square is a great place to buy these products. Look for Guinness-flavored toffees and Irish Porter cake. The Old Jameson Distillery sells all manner of Irish whiskey-flavored items—truffles, jams, fudge, chutney—but don't forget a bottle of the real thing.

Shopping by Theme

Whether you're looking for a department store, a quirky boutique, or something in between, you'll find it all in Dublin. On this page shops are listed by theme. For a more detailed write-up, see the individual listings in Dublin by Area.

Dublin by Night

Whether you like clubs, cocktail bars or traditional pubs, there is no shortage of venues. Dublin's theaters are famous. Big-name stars and hit musicals pack the massive O2 arena, and other venues feature a wide repertoire of plays and opera, or perhaps you prefer to catch one of the latest releases at the cinema.

Anyone for a Drink?

Dublin pubs are an institution and pub crawls make for a great night out, especially when you try to track down the thickest and tastiest pint of Guinness or Murphy's, or a lighter lager—Harp is brewed in Dublin. Although most pubs close at 11pm, 11.30pm or 12.30am, some pubs, bars and clubs serve alcohol late—until 2.30am on one or more nights. There is a smoking ban in all pubs. Watch out for leaflets detailing Irish music or jazz and rock sessions in many pubs and bars.

Laughter or Dancing?

Expanding fast, Dublin's comedy scene sees plenty of new talent emerging and comedy clubs seem to open all the time. There is stand-up comedy at many pubs every night; on open-mic nights comedians and other acts battle it out to be acclaimed as the night's best act. The Comedy Cellar at the International Bar on Wicklow Street hosts internationally renowned comedians and is famed for attracting rising stars. Dance clubs pulse with hardcore, garage, techno, electro, deep funk, house and chart toppers.

Cheers in Irish is sláinte. Have a traditional night out in a pub or go to one of Dublin's historic theaters

---

MERRION SQUARE

Evening light is kind to Dublin's Georgian architecture. Under illumination, the imposing buildings and elegant squares resemble the set of a magnificent period drama. Take an evening stroll around Merrion Square, down Merrion Street Upper and on to Baggot Street to see the dramatic sight of the illuminated National Museum and the Government Buildings.

ESSENTIAL DUBLIN   DUBLIN BY NIGHT

Eating Out

During Ireland's boom years, new restaurants and bars opened up at a bewildering rate, many of them extremely good. Young, talented Irish chefs transformed the menus, placing great emphasis on good-quality local ingredients, and the number of Michelin stars grew. The economic downturn has seen prices drop considerably, although eating out in Dublin is still not cheap.

What's on Offer?

Look for good-value lunch specials and 'pre-theatre' or 'early-bird' menus, served before 7pm, when even upscale restaurants become affordable. While the choice of dishes may be smaller, there's no dip in quality. The vast array of restaurants reflects Dublin's cosmopolitan character, from Mediterranean and European cuisines through Thai, Japanese, Chinese and Malaysian to Middle Eastern specialties. Wherever you eat, portions will be generous.

Irish Cooking

Many pubs still offer traditional fare but in restaurants and bistros, New Irish Cuisine has replaced the time-honored, rather heavy dishes. Innovative chefs are taking the country's fine, fresh ingredients and creating light, modern menus full of taste and stylishly presented.

Mealtimes

Breakfast may be served from 7am until 10am and lunch from 12 until 2.30pm, but with so many cafés, bistros and pubs open all day, finding something to suit is never a problem. Dinner is often served from around 5.30pm in restaurants and last orders could be at 10pm, but many ethnic restaurants keep later hours.

There is so much on offer in Dublin, from oyster bars to historic cafés to stylish and trendy eateries

---

DRESS CODE

As with most things in life, the Irish take a very laid-back approach to dress codes. Casual attire is fine in all but the most expensive restaurants and some of the smarter hotel restaurants.

Restaurants by Cuisine

There are restaurants to suit all tastes and budgets in Dublin. On this page they are listed by cuisine. For a more detailed description of each restaurant, see Dublin by Area.

CASUAL DINING

Bad Ass Café (▷ 42)
Bear (▷ 42)
Beat (▷ 42)
The Bank on College Green (▷ 85)
The Fumbally (▷ 43)
F.X. Buckley (▷ 43)
Gallaghers Boxty House (▷ 43)
Harbourmaster Bar & Restaurant (▷ 60)
Hatch & Sons Irish Kitchen (▷ 86)
MV *Cill Airne* (▷ 60)
Old Jameson Distillery (▷ 60)
The Shack (▷ 44)

COFFEE AND TEA

Avoca Cafés (▷ 106)
Bewley's Café (▷ 85)
The Gallery (▷ 86)
Panem (▷ 60)
Queen of Tarts (▷ 44)

ELEGANT DINING

Chapter One (▷ 60)
Dax (▷ 86)
L'Ecrivain (▷ 86)
Fire (▷ 86)
Les Frères Jacques (▷ 43)
Lobster Pot (▷ 106)
Marco Pierre White Steakhouse & Grill (▷ 87)
Pearl Brasserie (▷ 87)
Restaurant Patrick Guilbaud (▷ 88)
Saddle Room and Oyster Bar (▷ 88)
Thorntons (▷ 88)

INTERNATIONAL

777 (▷ 42)
Il Baccaro (▷ 42)
Bella Cuba (▷ 106)
Botticelli (▷ 42)
Café Topolis (▷ 42)
The Cedar Tree (▷ 42)
Chameleon (▷ 42)
Chi (▷ 106)
Chili Club (▷ 85)
Diep Le Shaker (▷ 86)
Dunne & Crescenzi (▷ 86)
Il Fornaio (▷ 60)
Langkawi (▷ 87)
La Mère Zou (▷ 87)
Mexico to Rome (▷ 44)
Mongolian Barbeque (▷ 44)
Monty's of Katmandu (▷ 44)
Pasta Fresca (▷ 87)
Saba (▷ 88)
Shanahan's on the Green (▷ 88)
Steps of Rome (▷ 88)
Thai Orchid (▷ 44)
Trastevere (▷ 44)
Wagamama (▷ 88)
Yamamori (▷ 44)

SNACKS

Cobalt Café (▷ 60)
Elephant and Castle (▷ 43)
Keoghs (▷ 86)
Lemon Crepe & Coffee Co. (▷ 43)
Odessa Lounge & Grill (▷ 44)

TRENDSETTERS

Bang Restaurant (▷ 85)
The Church (▷ 60)
Eden (▷ 43)
Hartley's (▷ 106)
The Farm (▷ 86)
Mao (▷ 87)
La Peniche (▷ 87)
Pichet (▷ 44)
The Pig's Ear (▷ 87)

VEGETARIAN/FISH

Beshoff's (▷ 60)
Cavistons (▷ 106)
Cornucopia (▷ 85)
Guinea Pig (The Fish Restaurant) (▷ 106)
King Sitric (▷ 106)
Leo Burdock (▷ 43)
Lord Edward (▷ 43)

Top Tops For...

However you'd like to spend your time in Dublin, these top suggestions should help you tailor your ideal visit. Each suggestion has a fuller write-up elsewhere in the book.

BEST IRISH BUYS

Brown Thomas department store (▷ 78) showcases established and up-and-coming Irish designers.
The Avoca (▷ 78) store is full of all things Irish and the food hall is brimming with tasty delights.
Waltons (▷ 38) is the place for your musical instruments Irish-style from bodhráns to whistles.

STYLE GURUS

Quirky and contemporary kitchen- and home-wares can be bought at Designist (▷ 37), created by designers Barbara Nolan and Jennie Flynn.
From kitchen to living room you should find something to suit you in Stock (▷ 81).
If it's fine art you are after go to former fashion designer Ib Jorgensen's gallery (▷ 79).

From traditonal to trendy—try some new tastes while you are in Dublin and you won't be disappointed

EASTERN DELIGHTS

For an informal dining experience take a trip to the Mongolian Barbeque (▷ 44), and create your own dish from the ingredients provided.
Try a sophisticated Thai eating experience at Diep Le Shaker (▷ 86).
Head for the popular Japanese restaurant Yamamori (▷ 44) for noodles and sushi.

FISHY BUSINESS

For a real fishy treat head to the exclusive Lord Edward restaurant (▷ 43).
DART out to Howth for the freshest of fish at the expensive, but worth it, King Sitric restaurant (▷ 106).
Down-to-earth fish and chips are at their best from Leo Burdock's takeout (▷ 43).

Elegant, fashionable but always maintaining the traditional in Dublin's fair city

STAYING AT A GEORGIAN TOWN HOUSE

Four town houses in one, the Merrion (▷ 112) is one of Dublin's most luxurious hotels—period elegance at its best.

Savor Georgian charm at the friendly Pembroke Townhouse (▷ 111) in leafy Dublin 4.

Relax at Staunton's on the Green (▷ 111), a calm oasis with a garden in the heart of the city.

FASHIONABLE NIGHTLIFE

Dress to impress at Lillie's Bordello (▷ 83) where celebs and the beautiful people hang out.

Pod (▷ 83) is a hip joint with a variety of sounds on different nights.

Opulence, big time, is on offer at the Café en Seine (▷ 82), a lively venue for cocktails and atmosphere.

TRADITIONAL MUSIC

Listen to Irish music every night upstairs at the Temple Bar pub, Oliver St. John Gogarty (▷ 40).

For impromptu music visit O'Donoghue's (▷ 83), one-time haunt of the Dubliners.

For dancing as well as music try O'Shea's Merchant (▷ 41) and be prepared for audience participation.

The musical heritage of Ireland is alive and kicking in pubs all over the city

THINGS FOR KIDS

Dublin Zoo (▷ 97) provides plenty of cuddly and not so cuddly animals to view.

Start on the road and then take to the water on a Viking Splash tour (▷ 77).

Thrill and enthrall them at the National Wax Museum Plus (▷ 35).

Dublinia (▷ 27) is a must for exploring Viking Dublin.

AN INEXPENSIVE TRIP

Getting away from city life is easy in Ireland's capital

Stay in a hostel—try Kinlay House (▷ 109).
Cornucopia vegetarian restaurant (▷ 85) offers a reasonably priced wholesome breakfast.
Stroll through the parks or Georgian squares, such as Merrion Square (▷ 75), it's free.

LUXURY TO BE SURE

Be pampered at the Dawson Hotel & Spa (▷ 112), with its gorgeous Mandala spa.
Dine at Ireland's leading French restaurant, Patrick Guilbaud (▷ 88).
Shop at Louise Kennedy (▷ 80) on Merrion Square for beautiful clothes and gifts.

THE GREAT OUTDOORS

Stroll in big Phoenix Park (▷ 98) or the less well-known peaceful Iveagh Gardens (▷ 74).
Take a trip on the DART (▷ 100–101) for great coast views and a breath of sea air.
Play a round of golf—the choice of courses is huge (▷ 105).

LITERARY GREATS

Find out about them all at the Dublin Writers Museum (▷ 50).
James Joyce is synonymous with Dublin, so get all the information on the great man at the James Joyce Centre (▷ 51).
Oscar Wilde reclines languidly on a rock in Merrion Square, while his house (▷ 76) is on the corner.
Visit the simple childhood home of one of Dublin's famous literary sons, George Bernard Shaw (▷ 35).

Green space is abundant in Dublin's gorgeous Georgian squares

Turn back the clock to another century at the home of the literary great, George Bernard Shaw

Dublin by Area

Although not the most attractive district of the city, the southwest area is one of the most historically interesting. From the early Celtic and Viking settlements, the medieval walled city of Dublin developed.

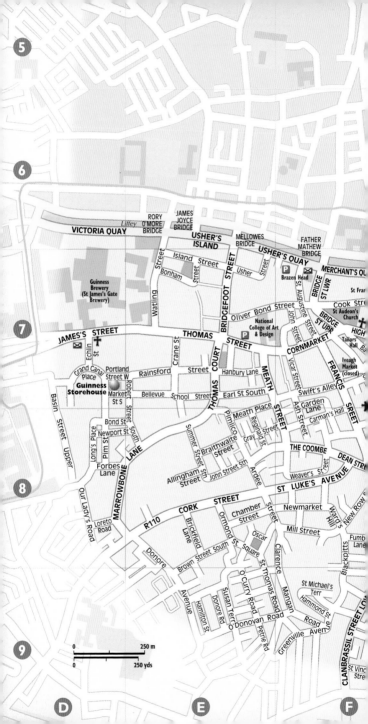

Bank of Ireland

Like a building from classical Greece, the Bank of Ireland also has stunning tapestries

THE BASICS

- ➕ H7
- ✉ 2 College Green
- ☎ 661 5933
- 🕐 House of Lords: Mon–Fri 10–3.30
- 🚆 Tara Street
- 🚌 Cross-city buses
- ♿ Few
- 🏛 Free
- ❓ Tours of House of Lords Tue 10.30, 11.30, 12.30

HIGHLIGHTS

- ● Exterior detail
- ● Former House of Lords with barrel-vaulted ceiling
- ● Jan van Beaver tapestries
- ● Crystal chandelier

This great semicircular building was the focus of Ireland's glorious years of freedom at the end of the 18th century, when the city reached the zenith of its architectural and artistic achievement.

Harmony The Bank of Ireland, overlooking College Green, began life as the upper and lower houses of the old Irish Parliament, which gained its legislative independence in 1782 but saw its members bribed to vote itself out of existence 18 years later. The world's first purpose-built Parliament House, its original architect was Edward Lovett Pearce, who designed the recessed south-facing 'piazza' of Ionic columns (c1729–39) and the rooms behind it, of which the old House of Lords is still intact and accessible to the public. It has a striking barrel-vaulted ceiling, a splendid oak and marble fireplace and features a wonderful Dublin crystal chandelier (1788) of 1,233 pieces, and two fine tapestries (1733) by Jan van Beaver—one of King James II at the 1689 Siege of Londonderry, the other of King William of Orange at the 1690 Battle of the Boyne.

Alterations The architect James Gandon added the curving and windowless screen and the east- and west-facing Corinthian porticos between 1785 and 1797. After the parliament was dissolved, the building was sold in 1802 to the Bank of Ireland, on condition that it be modified to prevent it from being used again for public debate. This was done by Francis Johnston and included the present banking rooms.

Hidden away behind the ivy, the Chester Beatty Library reveals its Chinese ceiling

Chester Beatty Library

American-born Sir Alfred Chester Beatty is one of the few people to have been made an honorary citizen of Ireland, a gesture made in gratitude for the rare and priceless art collection that he bequeathed to the nation in 1956.

Hidden treasure The library and Oriental art gallery named after its founder and benefactor, Sir Alfred Chester Beatty (1875–1968), is one of Dublin's jewels but often overlooked. The unique collection is displayed on two floors in a converted Georgian building.

Masterpieces Alfred Chester Beatty, a successful mining engineer born in New York and knighted for his services to Britain as an advisor to Winston Churchill during World War II, devoted an important part of his life to the search for manuscripts and objets d'art of the highest quality. The collections range from c2700BC up to the present day, and stretch geographically from Japan in the east to Europe in the west. Religious writings range from one of the earliest known New Testament papyri to the Korans, all masterpieces of calligraphy. There is a wealth of Persian and Mughal miniature paintings as well as wonders of the East such as Burmese and Siamese painted fairy-tale books or *parabaiks*, Chinese silk paintings and jade snuff bottles, and Japanese *netsuke* and woodblock prints. Permanent exhibitions are focused on two themes: Arts of the Book and Sacred Traditions. The library also stages temporary exhibitions.

THE BASICS

www.cbl.ie

🚉 G7

✉ Dublin Castle

☎ 407 0750

🕐 Mon–Fri 10–5 (closed Mon Oct–end Apr), Sat 11–5, Sun 1–5

🍴 Café

🚉 Tara Street

🚌 Cross-city buses

♿ Good

🎟 Free

❓ Audio-visual presentations. Free guided tours. Roof Garden

HIGHLIGHTS

● New Testament papyri
● Koran manuscripts
● Persian and Mughal paintings
● Jade snuff bottles

Christ Church Cathedral

TOP
25

The superb nave (left); Christ Church (middle); treasures in the Crypt (right)

THE BASICS

www.christchurchdublin.ie

➕ F7

✉ Christchurch Place

☎ 677 8099

🕐 Mar–end May Mon–Sat 9–6, Sun 12.30–2.30, 4.30–6.30; Jun–end Sep Mon–Sat 9–7, Sun 12.30–2.30, 4.30–7; Oct–end Feb Mon–Sat 9–5, Sun 12.30–2.30

🚌 49A, 50, 51B, 54A, 65, 77, 123

♿ Good

💶 Moderate

HIGHLIGHTS

● 12th-century south transept
● Leaning north wall
● Knight's effigy
● Crypt and 'Treasures of Christ Church'

Christ Church Cathedral is not only Dublin's oldest stone building but also perhaps the Normans' outstanding contribution to Irish architecture. It reflects 1,000 years of worship in Ireland.

History The older of Dublin's two cathedrals, Christ Church was founded by the Norse king Sitric Silkenbeard in 1038. The northern side of the choir and the south transept are the oldest parts of the existing stone structure and have been dated back to just before 1180. This indicates that work started on it shortly after the Normans took over the city, employing masons brought over from England. The early Gothic nave, dated c1226–36, also reflects English influence. Its vault collapsed in 1562, leaving the north wall with an outward lean of about 45cm (18in).

Restoration The whole building would now be a romantic ivied ruin but for the Dublin whiskey distiller Henry Roe, who paid for its reconstruction between 1871 and 1878. The work was carried out under the direction of the English Victorian architect George Edmund Street, who added flying buttresses to keep the whole edifice standing. Look for the effigy of a knight in armor near the entrance. It represents Strongbow, leader of the Anglo-Normans, who captured Dublin in 1170 and was buried in the cathedral in 1176. An unusual feature is the original crypt, extending the entire length of the cathedral and housing the Treasury. Exhibits include a mummified cat and mouse, plus a video of the cathedral's history.

Learn about life in medieval Dublin and meet the Vikings—but mind the stocks

Dublinia

If you want to know just what made Dublin's Viking and medieval ancestors tick, check out Dublinia with Viking exhibitions, reconstructions, audio-visual and interactive displays.

Vivid re-creation Dublinia, as the town was first recorded on a map *c*1540, is a vibrant re-creation of medieval Dublin life housed in the Victorian-era former Synod Hall. After the Vikings had re-established the city in this area during the 10th century, Hiberno-Norsemen and Normans occupied it from 1170 until the end of the Middle Ages—the time-span covered by Dublinia. The exhibition 'Viking World' reveals a fascinating glimpse of the Viking past and dispels many myths. The storyboards and talking heads are particularly good.

Excavations Over 30 years of excavations in the Dublinia area have uncovered many fascinating objects such as leatherwork, pottery decorated with amusing faces, floor tiles, jewelry and ships' timbers, which are also on view in the exhibition. An interesting audio-visual presentation of the city's history complements the series of life-size model tableaux that illustrate episodes from the past. 'History Hunters' is an exciting exhibition that uncovers the world of archaeology. The display showing the reconstruction of a 900-year-old Dublin woman's face is amazing. To complete your visit, climb the 96 steps in the tower of 15th-century St. Michael's Church, incorporated into the Synod Hall when it was built, for views of the city and river.

THE BASICS

www.dublinia.ie

⊞ F7

✉ St. Michael's Hill, Christchurch

☎ 679 4611

🕐 Mar–end Sep daily 10–5 (last admission 4.15); Oct–end Feb daily 10–4.30 (last admission 4)

🚌 50, 51B, 78A

🍴 Café

♿ Dublinia: good. Tower and bridge: none

💶 Moderate

❓ Prebookable tours. Wheelchair accessible

HIGHLIGHTS

● Re-creation of medieval Dublin
● Archaeology
● Interactive re-created Medieval Fair
● Viking re-creations
● View over Dublin

Dublin Castle

- Powder Tower
- State Apartments
- Chapel Room

How many buildings in Europe can claim to have been the hub of a country's secular power for longer than Dublin Castle, the headquarters of English rule in Ireland for more than 700 years?

Ancient site Dublin Castle, now used for State occasions, presidential inaugurations and occasional European summit meetings, stands on the site of a much older Viking settlement. It occupies the southeastern corner of the Norman walled town overlooking the long-vanished black pool or *dubh linn* that gave the city its ancient Irish name. The castle's defined rectangular shape was determined from the start in 1204 with the construction of a twin-towered entrance on the north side and stout circular bastions at each corner. The excavated remains of one of these,

Clockwise from far left: The red drawing room at Dublin Castle; the elegant throne room; the facade of the castle has seen many alterations over the centuries; a fountain in the castle grounds; a ceiling painting in St. Patrick's Hall; a depiction of the Great Courtyard dating from 1792

the Powder Tower, shown on the guided tour, rested on an earlier Viking foundation and was attached to the city wall beside an arch, beneath which water flowed from the old castle moat.

Interior After a fire in 1684, the interior was almost entirely rebuilt in the 18th and early 19th centuries. On the south side of Upper Castle Yard are the State Apartments, where the English king's viceroy lived until the castle was handed over to the Irish State in 1922. These regal rooms form the second half of the guided tour, which starts in the Powder Tower.

City Hall Next door to the castle is the imposing City Hall with its exhibition, 'The Story of the Capital' (Mon–Sat 10–5.15). Check out the fabulous ceilings in the entrance hall.

THE BASICS

www.dublincastle.ie

✚ G7

✉ Dame Street

☎ 677 7129

🕐 Mon–Sat 9.45–4.45, Sun and public hols 12–4.15. State Apartments closed occasionally for functions

🍴 Restaurant/café

🚆 Tara Street

🚌 Cross-city buses

♿ State Apartments: good. Powder Tower: none

💶 Moderate

❓ Gardens, open Mon–Fri, not part of tour

Guinness Storehouse

TOP
25

HIGHLIGHTS

- Glass pint structure
- Brewing exhibition
- Transportation section
- Classic advertisements and memorabilia
- Rooftop view

TIPS

- The admission fee includes a complimentary pint of Guinness.
- Check out the flagship shop selling Guinness merchandise and memorabilia.

Think Dublin, think Guinness. For 250 years, the 'black stuff' has been an integral part of the city's economy and history. Today, the Guinness Storehouse is Ireland's No. 1 visitor attraction.

What's in a glass? The massive steel beams and powerful Guinness 'surge' in the Atrium are a perfect introduction to this 1904 building. At its core is what is described as a 'giant' pint glass. Within this glass structure your journey through the production process of a pint of Guinness begins. Simple, dramatic displays show the four basic ingredients—hops, barley, yeast and water—all of which you can touch, feel and smell. The displays provoke the senses as indicated on the huge wall label reading 'Smells are delectable too, the heavy sleepy scent of hops—steam, hot metal, sweat'.

Take a drink in the Gravity Bar, which offers one of the finest views of Dublin (left); the Guinnness Storehouse illuminated at night—an icon of Dublin's economy, past and present (right)

Mine's a pint You follow the pint as it makes its way through the brewery of the past, founded by Arthur Guinness in 1759—a past still much in evidence today. Old machinery is cleverly utilized, doubling up as interactives to give you more information. From the brewing process you go to the transportation section, with large-scale models showing how Guinness has reached the far-flung corners of the world. The advertising display is great fun, with popular memorabilia and a hall of fame recalling classic Guinness advertisements. You learn how Guinness has affected many aspects of Irish life as a supporter of the arts, festivals and sport, then finish your journey at the top of the glass, in the Gravity Bar, with a splendid view over Dublin and your free pint. Every year more than a million people visit the Storehouse, making it Ireland's most popular attraction.

THE BASICS

www.guinness-storehouse.com

🛡 D7

✉ St. James's Gate

☎ 408 4800

🕙 Daily 9.30–5 (until 7 in Jul, Aug)

🍴 Brewery Bar, Gravity Bar, Source Bar

🚌 51B, 78A from Aston Quay; 123 from O'Connell Street; Luas St. James's

♿ Excellent

💷 Expensive

❓ Shop

Marsh's Library

The oldest public library in Ireland is light years away from modern Dublin

THE BASICS

www.marshlibrary.ie

➕ G8

✉ St. Patrick's Close

☎ 454 3511

🕐 Mon, Wed–Fri 9.30–1, 2–5, Sat 10–1

🚌 Cross-city buses

♿ Few

👆 Inexpensive

HIGHLIGHTS

● Old-world atmosphere
● Oak bookcases
● 'Cages' for rare works
● Books and manuscripts

This magnificent example of an 18th-century scholar's library has changed little since it opened 300 years ago. One of the few buildings here to retain its original purpose, it remains a calm oasis of scholarly learning.

Rare legacy In 1701, Archbishop Narcissus Marsh (1638–1713) built Ireland's first public library close to St. Patrick's Cathedral and filled it with his own books. In 1705 he accquired 10,000 more, purchased from the Bishop of Worcester. Two years later, the library was given official legal standing when the Irish parliament passed an Act for 'settling and preserving a public library'. The building is one of the city's rare legacies from the reign of Queen Anne and was designed by Sir William Robinson, responsible for the Royal Hospital at Kilmainham (▷ 94–95), using distinctive gray Dublin limestone on one side and red brick on the front.

Precious books Inside, the long gallery is flanked on each side by dark oak bookcases topped by carvings of an archbishop's miter. At the end of the L-shaped gallery are three alcoves, or 'cages', where readers were locked with the library's precious books. As an extra safeguard, chains were attached to the books (though not to the readers). Some 25,000 volumes fill the shelves. In a wide range of subjects and languages, they span the 15th to the early 18th centuries. The library also possesses some 300 manuscripts, including Elizabethan lute tablature music.

St. Patrick's Cathedral (left); bust of Jonathan Swift (middle); detail on a tomb (right)

TOP 25

St. Patrick's Cathedral

'Here is laid the body of Jonathan Swift, Doctor of Divinity, Dean of this Cathedral Church, where fierce indignation can no longer rend the heart. Go traveller, and imitate, if you can, this earnest and dedicated champion of liberty.'

Literary connections Jonathan Swift's epitaph is a fitting tribute to the personality most often associated with St. Patrick's Cathedral. The author of *Gulliver's Travels*—written as a political satire but enjoyed by generations of children—Swift was the cathedral's fearless and outspoken Dean from 1713 until his death in 1745. He and his beloved friend, Stella, are buried in the south aisle.

History Founded in 1191 near a sacred well where St. Patrick is said to have baptized pagans, Ireland's national cathedral was built in Early English Gothic style and completed by 1284. Like Christ Church (▷ 26), St. Patrick's was heavily restored in the 19th century, with funds from the Guinness family. The cathedral embodies the history and heritage of the Irish people and receives over 300,000 visitors and pilgrims every year.

Monuments Look for the tomb and effigy of the 17th-century adventurer Richard Boyle, Earl of Cork, and a memorial to the Irish bard and harpist Turlough O'Carolan (1670–1738). In the south choir aisle are two of Ireland's rare 16th-century monumental brasses. George Frederick Handel practiced on the cathedral's organ before the first public performance of his *Messiah* in 1742.

THE BASICS

www.stpatrickscathedral.ie

✚ F8

✉ St. Patrick's Close

☎ 453 9472

🕐 Mar–end Oct Mon–Fri 9–5, Sat 9–6, Sun 9–10.30, 12.30–2.30, 4.30–6; Nov–end Feb Mon–Sat 9–5, Sun 9–10.30, 12.30–4.30. Visiting restricted during services

🚌 Cross-city buses

♿ Good

💷 Moderate

❓ Living Stones exhibition explores St. Patrick's history. Guided tour (free) Mon–Sat 11.30, 2.30 .

HIGHLIGHTS

● Swift's bust and epitaph
● Medieval brasses
● Memorial to O'Carolan
● Organ
● Living Stones exhibition

THE SOUTHWEST TOP 25

33

Temple Bar

TOP 25

Traditional music at Oliver St. John Gogarty (left); advertising the 'black stuff' (right)

THE BASICS

www.templebar.ie

➕ G7

✉ Temple Bar Information Centre, 12 East Essex Street, Temple Bar

☎ 677 2255

🚉 Tara Street

🚌 Cross-city buses

Meeting House Square

➕ G7

✉ Temple Bar

🚉 Tara Street

🚌 Cross-city buses

HIGHLIGHTS

● Meeting House Square
● Pubs, bars and cafés
● Markets: food (Sat 10–4.30 ▷ 38) in Meeting House Square; books (Sat, Sun 11–6) in Temple Bar Square
● Street theater

The area known as Temple Bar lies between Dame Street and the River Liffey and covers some 11ha (27 acres). It takes its name from the Anglo-Irish aristocrat, Sir William Temple, who owned land here in the 17th century. In Viking times it was the heart of the city.

Early beginnings Business flourished in Temple Bar from the early 17th century but the area fell into decline in the early 20th century and by the late 1980s had been proposed as the site for a new bus terminal. Objections were vociferous and the city's 'left bank' began to take off.

Dublin's Cultural Quarter Today, pedestrian-friendly and with restricted vehicle access, this is a vibrant cultural district and the main draw for tourists with its mix of restaurants, shops, markets, pubs and bars. It is the venue for artists' studios, print galleries, theater and music. Temple Bar's popularity has meant that at times there has been unwanted unruly behavior. It does still get rowdy at weekends, but during the day and on weekday nights it is great fun to be in. Nearby Cow's Lane, Dublin's oldest district and redeveloped in 2004, is the setting for Designer Mart, featuring innovative designers, held every Saturday.

Meeting House Square In the heart of Temple Bar, this square is the focus for performance art, the summer open-air cinema and the wonderful Saturday market (▷ panel 38). This is a showcase for Irish talent be it art, music or juggling.

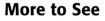

THE ARK

www.ark.ie

This specially created cultural venue for children of all ages offers around 10 delightful art and culture events each year. There are regular plays and music workshops, but check for details as many of the events are for school groups only.

🔴 G7 ✉ 11a Eustace Street ☎ 670 7788 🚊 Tara Street 🚌 Cross-city buses 🦽 Good 👆 Depends on activity

THE NATIONAL WAX MUSEUM PLUS

www.waxmuseumplus.ie

Step through Irish history and a scary Chamber of Horrors at this hugely popular venue—a snapshot of cultural heritage. See lifelike wax models of Irish actors, famous musicians and sporting legends, and even make your own video to upload online. There's also a science and invention zone, with interactive exhibits, paying homage to Ireland's top inventors and scientists.

🔴 H7 ✉ 4 Foster Place, Temple Bar ☎ 671 8373 🕐 Daily 10–7 🚊 Tara Street 🚌 Cross-city buses 👆 Expensive

SHAW'S BIRTHPLACE

The 'author of many plays' reads the plaque outside the childhood home of playwright George Bernard Shaw (1856–1950). It is full of Victorian charm, and due to reopen in early 2015.

🔴 G9 ✉ 33 Synge Street ☎ 475 0854 🕐 Check for opening hours before visiting 🚌 16, 16A, 19 🦽 Few 👆 Moderate

WHITEFRIAR STREET CARMELITE CHURCH

www.carmelites.ie

Full of shrines, Whitefriar's contains the relics of St. Valentine. It's one of the largest churches in Dublin and the altar holds the medieval carved oak Madonna and Child, known as 'Our Lady of Dublin'.

🔴 G8 ✉ 56 Aungier Street ☎ 475 8821 🕐 Mon, Wed–Fri 7.45–6, Tue 7.45–9.15, Sat–Sun 7.45–7.30 🚊 Pearse 🚌 Cross-city buses 🦽 Good 👆 Free

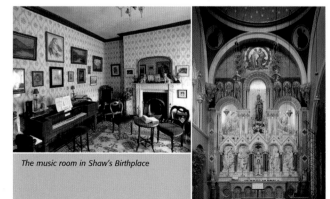

The music room in Shaw's Birthplace

Shrine in Whitefriar Street Carmelite Church

Walk Along the Quays

The English-born architect James Gandon (1743–1823) played an important role in the beautification of Dublin.

DISTANCE: 1.5km (1 mile) **ALLOW:** 45 minutes

START

GEORGE'S QUAY
✚ J6 🚌 Cross-city buses

END

FOUR COURTS (▷ 54)
✚ F6 🚌 Cross-city buses

THE SOUTHWEST WALK

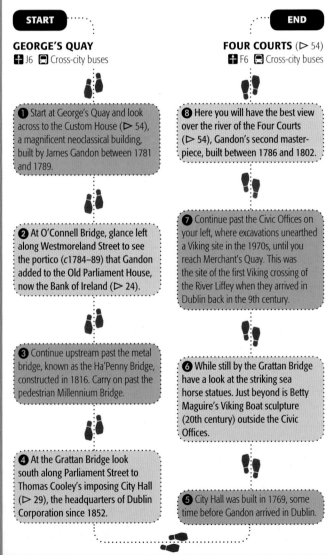

❶ Start at George's Quay and look across to the Custom House (▷ 54), a magnificent neoclassical building, built by James Gandon between 1781 and 1789.

❷ At O'Connell Bridge, glance left along Westmoreland Street to see the portico (c1784–89) that Gandon added to the Old Parliament House, now the Bank of Ireland (▷ 24).

❸ Continue upstream past the metal bridge, known as the Ha'Penny Bridge, constructed in 1816. Carry on past the pedestrian Millennium Bridge.

❹ At the Grattan Bridge look south along Parliament Street to Thomas Cooley's imposing City Hall (▷ 29), the headquarters of Dublin Corporation since 1852.

❽ Here you will have the best view over the river of the Four Courts (▷ 54), Gandon's second master-piece, built between 1786 and 1802.

❼ Continue past the Civic Offices on your left, where excavations unearthed a Viking site in the 1970s, until you reach Merchant's Quay. This was the site of the first Viking crossing of the River Liffey when they arrived in Dublin back in the 9th century.

❻ While still by the Grattan Bridge have a look at the striking sea horse statues. Just beyond is Betty Maguire's Viking Boat sculpture (20th century) outside the Civic Offices.

❺ City Hall was built in 1769, some time before Gandon arrived in Dublin.

Shopping

CLADDAGH RECORDS
www.claddaghrecords.com
Specialist music shop
hidden away in a Temple
Bar backstreet. It sells
CDs and DVDs from the
countrified sound of Irish
dance bands to the archly
traditional and contem-
porary. The staff know
their stuff.
🔲 G7 ✉ 2 Cecilia Street,
Temple Lane ☎ 677 0262
🚉 Tara Street 🚌 Cross-city
buses

COW'S LANE
DESIGNER STUDIO
www.cowslanedesignerstudio.ie
Buy fashion, knits, jewelry
and homewares from
this Dublin-based design
collective. On Saturdays,
visit the outdoor Designer
Mart in Cow's Lane.
🔲 G7 ✉ Essex Street West,
Temple Bar ☎ 524 0001
🚉 Tara Street 🚌 Cross-city
buses

DESIGN CENTRE
www.designcentre.ie
A boutique collection
inside the Powerscourt
Centre (▷ 38), with
fashion from renowned
Irish and international
designers. Look out for
accessories from Irish
designer Philip Treacy.
🔲 H7 ✉ Powerscourt
Centre, 59 South William
Street ☎ 677 1413
🚉 Pearse 🚌 Cross-city
buses

DESIGNIST
www.designist.ie
Created by designers
Barbara Nolan and Jennie

Flynn, this new store sells
a collection of contempo-
rary kitchen- and home-
wares, quirky jewelry and
cool-as-you-like Dublin-
themed ornaments.
🔲 G7 ✉ 68 South Great
George's Street ☎ 475 8534
🚉 Pearse 🚌 Cross-city buses

EAGER BEAVER
Buy vintage second-hand
clothes and accessories
for men and women,
ranging from denim
jackets to party dresses
and flannel shirts.
🔲 G7 ✉ 17 Crown Alley,
Temple Bar ☎ 677 3342
🚉 Tara Street 🚌 Cross-city
buses

FLIP
www.flipclothing.com
This Temple Bar shop is
one of the first ports
of call for trendy Irish
shoppers on the trail
of vintage second-hand

clothing from Europe and
America. They have their
own label, too.
🔲 G7 ✉ 3–4 Fownes
Street Upper, Temple Bar
☎ 671 4299 🚉 Tara Street
🚌 Cross-city buses

GEORGE'S STREET
ARCADE
www.georgesstreetarcade.ie
This covered, Victorian
shopping arcade, Ireland's
oldest, has an eclectic
array of shops and stalls.
You'll find everything from
vintage clothes at Retro
and second-hand vinyl
at Spindizzy Records to
tempting gourmet food at
Lolly & Cooks.
🔲 G7 ✉ Between South
Great George's Street and
Drury Street 🚉 Pearse
🚌 Cross-city buses

HARLEQUIN
Classy vintage clothing
and accessories, in
particular vintage hand-
bags, which are a house
specialty.
🔲 G7 ✉ 13 Castle Market
☎ 671 0202 🚉 Pearse
🚌 Cross-city buses

JENNY VANDER
The place for intricate
evening wear, coats,
dresses and separates
in delicate and luxurious
fabrics as well as shoes,
handbags and jewelry
from another era. The
clothes are all more
antique than second-
hand.
🔲 G7 ✉ 50 Drury Street
☎ 677 0406
🚌 Cross-city buses

BURIED TREASURE

Although Dubliners tend to
be hoarders by nature, the
city has always had a great
choice of antique, vintage
and second-hand clothing
stores. If you are lucky, you
can uncover genuine
treasures in these shops, at
market stalls and in the
city's numerous charity
shops. In fact, some items
may have been rented or
loaned out to wardrobe
departments on film sets,
so you could be buying a
celebrity cast off.

THE SOUTHWEST SHOPPING

JOHN FARRINGTON ANTIQUES

This small shop is packed to the gills with Irish furniture, silver, glass and objets d'art. The precious antique jewelry is fabulous. Celebrity clientele.
✚ G7 ✉ 32 Drury Street
☎ 679 1899 🚊 Pearse
🚌 Cross-city buses

MCCULLOUGH PIGOTT

www.mcculloughpigott.com
Highly respected by music lovers who while away the time gazing at the musical instruments and browsing through the sheet music.
✚ G7 ✉ 11 William Street
☎ 677 3138 🚊 Pearse
🚌 Cross-city buses

O'SULLIVAN ANTIQUES

www.osullivanantiques.com
A seasoned expert on the Irish antiques scene, Chantal O'Sullivan has a keen eye for exquisite items from years gone by. Mahogany furniture, gilt mirrors, marble mantelpieces, garden statues and delicate glass.
✚ F7 ✉ 43–44 Francis Street ☎ 454 1143
🚌 78A, 123

PATAGONIA

www.patagonia.com
Their first outlet shop in Europe is in a Georgian building close to Grafton Street. Iconic brand of eco-friendly outdoor wear with bargains on the previous season's gear.
✚ G7 ✉ 24–26 Exchequer Street ☎ 670 5748
🚌 Cross-city buses

PEEKABOO

www.peekaboodublin.com
For the dress for that special occasion, this shop makes made-to-order beautiful garments in gorgeous materials. Also some ready-to-wear.
✚ G7 ✉ 18 Lower Liffey Street ☎ 283 5232
🚊 Ormond Quay 🚌 Cross-city buses

POWERSCOURT CENTRE

www.powerscourtcentre.ie
A warren of boutiques, gift and craft stores, restaurants, cafés and art galleries within a Georgian town house. The Design Centre (▷ 37) is well worth a look. Good place for a coffee break.
✚ H7 ✉ 59 South William Street ☎ 679 4144
🚊 Pearse 🚌 Cross-city buses

TEMPLE BAR TRADING COMPANY

www.thetemplebarpub.com
This shop sells all the usual Irish souvenirs plus some interesting local art, Irish books and CDs.
✚ G7 ✉ 43–44 Temple Bar
☎ 670 3527 🚊 Tara Street
🚌 Cross-city buses

TIMEPIECE ANTIQUE CLOCKS

www.timepieceantiqueclocks.com
Both selling and restoration goes on at this intriguing shop that is all about 18th- and 19th-century clocks. The emphasis is on Irish longcase clocks but there are some highly decorative French pieces as well.
✚ F8 ✉ 58 Patrick Street
☎ 454 0774
🚌 Cross-city buses

WALTONS

www.waltons.ie
Dublin brims over with music and musicians, and Waltons supplies everyone from wannabe rock stars to the stalwarts of the traditional scene. They have been Irish music specialists for more than 75 years. From bodhráns to whistles, pipes to accordions, plus sheet music, Irish songbooks and accessories.
✚ G7 ✉ 69–70 South Great George's Street
☎ 475 0661 🚊 Pearse
🚌 Cross-city buses

SATURDAY MARKET

Irish food lovers spend Saturday in Meeting House Square at Temple Bar, where the weekly food market sells a variety of produce ranging from Japanese sushi to Mexican *burritos*. Local Irish produce includes fresh breads, jams, yogurts and vegetables. Those with a sweeter tooth will enjoy the handmade fudge and chocolate stalls or freshly cooked waffles and crêpes. Cheeses, olives, oysters and more.

Entertainment and Nightlife

ANDREW'S LANE
www.andrewslanetheatre.com
The 220-seat main stage and a smaller 76-seat studio upstairs attract young theatergoers.
🚇 H7 ✉ 12–16 Andrew's Lane ☎ 679 5720 🚉 Pearse
🚌 Cross-city buses

BRAZEN HEAD
www.brazenhead.com
Reputedly the oldest bar in town (trading for more than 800 years), the Brazen Head has an old-world charm. Good food, drink and Irish music sessions.
🚇 F7 ✉ 20 Bridge Street Lower ☎ 679 5186 🚌 121

BUTTON FACTORY
www.buttonfactory.ie
In the Temple Bar Music Centre, a premier music venue with club nights and dancehall events.
🚇 G7 ✉ Curved Street, Temple Bar ☎ 670 9202
🚉 Tara Street 🚌 Cross-city buses

CLUB M
www.clubm.ie
A lively club in the heart of Temple Bar with galleries, chill-out zones and a champagne VIP bar. Varied sounds into the early hours.
🚇 H7 ✉ Cope Street, Temple Bar ☎ 671 5622
🚉 Tara Street
🚌 Cross-city buses

FITZSIMONS
www.fitzsimonshotel.com
Popular party venue and happening nightspot.

The nightclub has theme nights, and DJs play a range of music. Major sporting events are shown on big screen TV. Live music every night in bars ranging over four floors. There is a roof terrace.
🚇 G7 ✉ 21–22 Wellington Quay, Temple Bar ☎ 677 9315 🚉 Tara Street
🚌 Cross-city buses

THE FRONT LOUNGE
www.thefrontlounge.ie
This stylish bar attracts a mixed crowd: business types by day, arty crowd by evening and gay and straight twentysomethings late at night.
🚇 G7 ✉ 33–34 Parliament Street ☎ 670 4112 🚉 Tara Street 🚌 Cross-city buses

HOGAN'S
A fashionable bar packed with Dublin's beautiful young things on their way to nearby dance clubs.
🚇 G7 ✉ 35 South Great George's Street ☎ 677 5904
🚌 Cross-city buses

STAR TURN

There's no shortage of big international names appearing in Dublin. When it comes to the live music scene, the city's major concert venues such as The O2 and the Ambassador have featured major stars, including Robbie Williams, Neil Diamond, Rod Stewart, and Westlife, on their schedules. You will need to book well in advance.

IRISH FILM INSTITUTE
www.ifi.ie
Art-house cinema showing independent Irish and international films. Occasional free events and curated seasons. Also an informal bar/restaurant, plus shop with film-related books, posters and DVDs.
🚇 G7 ✉ 6 Eustace Street, Temple Bar ☎ 679 5744
🚉 Tara Street 🚌 Cross-city buses

THE LONG HALL
Time seems to have stood still in this traditional hostelry, with a long bar, smoked glass and lovely paintwork.
🚇 G7 ✉ 51 South Great George's Street ☎ 475 1590
🚌 Cross-city buses

THE NEW THEATRE
www.thenewtheatre.com
Through the Connolly Bookshop, this venue for drama showcases new Irish work.
🚇 G7 ✉ 43 Essex Street East, Temple Bar ☎ 670 3361 🚉 Tara Street
🚌 Cross-city buses

OLIVER ST. JOHN GOGARTY
www.gogartys.ie
A pub since the mid-19th century, in the heart of Temple Bar, popular for traditonal music. Good food and great craic.
🚇 H6 ✉ 58–59 Fleet Street
☎ 671 1822 🕙 Music daily
🚉 Tara Street
🚌 Cross-city buses

OLYMPIA
www.olympia.ie
Dublin's oldest theater
attracts singers, musicians,
stage shows, comedy and
pantomimes.
➕ G7 ✉ 72 Dame Street
☎ 679 3323 🚉 Tara Street
🚌 Cross-city buses

O'SHEA'S MERCHANT
www.themerchanttemplebar.
com
Nightly traditional music
and dancing—everyone
is encouraged to take to
the dance floor. Let your
inhibitions go.
➕ F7 ✉ 12 Bridge Street
Lower ☎ 679 3797
🚌 51B, 78

PALACE BAR
www.thepalacebardublin.com
Established in 1843, this
traditional pub still retains
its old frosted glass and
mahogany interior. It
was a preferred haunt
of many literary giants
of Dublin including Brendan
Behan, Patrick Kavanagh
and W. B. Yeats.
➕ H6 ✉ 21 Fleet Street
☎ 671 7388 🚌 Cross-city
buses

THE PORTERHOUSE
www.porterhousebrewco.com
This was Dublin's first
microbrewery and,
despite new competition,
is still doing an excellent
job. It brews four ales,
three stouts, three lagers
and the occasional
special on the premises,
and stocks a huge
selection of bottled beers.
The Cook House on the

second and third floors
serves good food, and
there's live music nightly.
➕ G7 ✉ 16–18 Parliament
Street, Temple Bar ☎ 679
8847 🚌 Cross-city buses

PROJECT ARTS
CENTRE
www.projectartscentre.ie
From visual arts to dance,
music and theater, in two
performance spaces and
a gallery. A chance for
Irish talent to shine.
➕ G7 ✉ 39 East Essex
Street ☎ 881 9613 🚉 Tara
Street 🚌 Cross-city buses

RÍ RÁ
www.rira.ie
DJs at this fun late-night
hangout play a range of
music. The upstairs Globe
Bar is more relaxing.
➕ G7 ✉ Dame Court
☎ 671 1220 🚉 Tara Street
🚌 Cross-city buses

MOVIE FACTS
● Dublin has one of the
highest per capita movie
attendances in Europe.
● The Irish Film Institute, the
Savoy and the Screen are all
venues for the Dublin film
festival in March.
● It's cheaper during the day.
● New films are sometimes
released earlier in Ireland
than in the UK due to the
film distribution system.
● On Saturday nights from
June to September there
are free showings of films
at Meeting House Square in
Temple Bar.

SMOCK ALLEY
http://smockalley.com
Dublin's first Theatre
Royal opened on this
site in 1662, entertaining
Dubliners until its closure
in 1787. The building
was converted into a
church but reopened as
a theater in 2012 after
extensive renovation. It
now stages contemporary
drama in its movable
200-seat theater, and
is home to the Gaiety
School of Acting.
➕ G7 ✉ 6–7 Exchange
Street Lower ☎ 677 0014
🚉 Pearse 🚌 Cross-city
buses

STAG'S HEAD
www.thestagshead.ie
Built in 1770 and
restyled in 1895, this pub
has retained wonderful
stained-glass windows,
wood carvings and iron
work. Attractively set off
a cobblestoned lane. Live
music; food.
➕ G7 ✉ 1 Dame Court
☎ 679 3687 🚉 Tara Street
🚌 Cross-city buses

WHELAN'S
www.whelanslive.com
Good acoustics, plenty of
space and a great atmos-
phere. Up-and-coming
Irish groups and overseas
bands often headline.
Licensed to serve alcohol
since 1772. Extensive
renovation work in 1989
revealed the original
wood and stonework.
➕ G8 ✉ 25 Wexford Street
☎ 478 0766 🚉 Pearse
🚌 16, 16A, 19, 19A, 65, 83

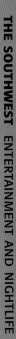

Restaurants

777 (€–€€)
www.777.ie
A fun new Mexican tapas restaurant and bar serving up authentic dishes such as beef *ennegrecido* and chorizo *taquitos*, with a family meal and also a special Sunday brunch. Fabulous cocktails in the bar.
➕ G7 ✉ 7 Castle House, South Great George's Street ☎ 425 4052 🕐 Lunch, dinner daily 🚌 Cross-city buses

IL BACCARO (€€)
www.ilbaccarodublin.com
Atmospheric *osteria* in a 17th-century vaulted cellar. Authentic Italian fare and great wines straight from the barrel.
➕ G7 ✉ Meeting House Square ☎ 671 4597 🕐 Lunch Tue–Sun 🚇 Tara Street 🚌 Cross-city buses

BAD ASS CAFÉ (€)
www.badassdublin.com
At this long-established pizza, pasta and burger restaurant, vegetarians and children are well catered to as well.
➕ G7 ✉ 9–11 Crown Alley, Temple Bar ☎ 675 3005 🕐 Daily 🚇 Tara Street 🚌 Cross-city buses

BEAR (€–€€)
www.joburger.ie
A branch of the popular Jo'Burger group, loved for its steaks with unusual salads, sides and sauces, all made using Irish ingredients. The rustic bar serves craft beers.
➕ G7 ✉ 34–35 South William Street ☎ 474 4888 🕐 Lunch and dinner daily 🚌 Cross-city buses

BOTTICELLI (€€)
www.botticelli.ie
An Italian restaurant run by Italians, serving good honest pizza, pasta, and meat and fish dishes from imported Italian ingredients. Book in advance for a table overlooking the river.
➕ G7 ✉ 3 Temple Bar ☎ 672 7289 🕐 Lunch and dinner daily 🚇 Tara Street 🚌 Cross-city buses

CAFÉ TOPOLIS (€€)
Good wholesome Italian fare, with pizzas cooked on a wood fire for authenticity. Choose from a large selection of pastas, salads, fish and meat dishes.
➕ G7 ✉ 37 Parliament Street, Temple Bar ☎ 670 4961 🕐 Lunch and dinner daily 🚇 Tara Street 🚌 Cross-city buses

THE CEDAR TREE (€€)
Middle Eastern setting with authentic Lebanese dishes and *meze*. Belly-dancing Saturday nights.
➕ H7 ✉ 11 St. Andrew's Street ☎ 677 2121 🕐 Dinner only 🚇 Pearse 🚌 Cross-city buses

CHAMELEON (€€)
www.chameleonrestaurant.com
The house specialty at this excellent restaurant is Dutch-Indonesian *rijsttafel*. Vegetarian, fish and coeliac menus are also served.
➕ G7 ✉ 1 Lower Fownes Street, Temple Bar ☎ 671 0362 🕐 Lunch Sat, dinner Tue–Sat from 5pm 🚇 Tara Street 🚌 Cross-city buses

CLEAVER EAST (€€€)
www.theclarence.ie
Irish chef Oiver Dunne has created a menu of sharing dishes and tasting plates celebrating local ingredients. Inside the elegant Clarence hotel, owned by Bono.
➕ G7 ✉ The Clarence, 6–8 Wellington Quay ☎ 531 3500 🕐 Lunch and dinner daily 🚌 Cross-city buses

EDEN (€€)

www.edenbarandgrill.ie
Enjoy modern Irish food with a Mediterranean slant in this contemporary restaurant with a huge stained-glass ceiling. Live music on Friday and Saturday evenings.
➕ H7 ✉ 7 South William Street ☎ 670 6887
🕐 Lunch and dinner daily
🚋 Pearse 🚌 Cross-city buses

ELEPHANT AND CASTLE (€€)

www.elephantandcastle.ie
A popular place, serving one of Dublin's largest breakfast and brunch menus, with American and European favorites. Expect to wait in line for a table, especially on Sundays.
➕ G7 ✉ 18 Temple Bar ☎ 679 3121 🕐 Breakfast/brunch, lunch and dinner daily
🚋 Tara Street 🚌 Cross-city buses

LES FRÈRES JACQUES (€€€)

www.lesfreresjacques.com
Excellent French cooking in a stylish but informal setting. The friendly owner and staff are happy to offer advice on the exquisite menu and wines. Centrally located.
➕ G7 ✉ 74 Dame Street ☎ 679 4555 🕐 Lunch Mon–Fri, dinner Mon–Sat
🚌 Cross-city buses

THE FUMBALLY (€)

www.thefumbally.ie
A group of food-loving friends set up this informal café, popular for its excellent coffee and mainly organic daily menu. Irish breakfast, Middle Eastern wraps, fresh soups and home-made cakes are on offer.
➕ F8 ✉ Fumbally Lane ☎ 529 8732 🕐 Breakfast and lunch (till 5pm) Mon–Sat
🚌 Cross-city buses

F.X. BUCKLEY (€€€)

www.fxbuckley.ie
The Temple Bar branch of this meat eater's heaven; but there's seafood as well. Locally sourced, free-range meats.
➕ G7 ✉ 2 Crow Street, Temple Bar ☎ 671 1248
🕐 Dinner daily 🚋 Tara Street 🚌 Cross-city buses

GALLAGHERS BOXTY HOUSE (€€)

www.boxtyhouse.ie
Traditional food focused

around the boxty, an Irish potato pancake with a choice of fillings such as meat, fish or vegetables. Well known for the tasty, but unusual, Baileys and brown-bread ice cream.
➕ G7 ✉ 20–21 Temple Bar ☎ 677 2762 🕐 Lunch and dinner daily 🚋 Tara Street
🚌 Cross-city buses

LEMON CREPE & COFFEE CO. (€)

www.lemonco.ie
Head here for mouth-watering crêpes, and wash them down with some great coffees—cappuccinos et al.
➕ G7 ✉ 66 South William Street ☎ 672 9044 🕐 Daily from 8am
🚋 Pearse 🚌 Cross-city buses

LEO BURDOCK (€)

www.leoburdock.com
Near Christ Church Cathedral, this Dublin institution sells excellent fish and chips which can be eaten across the road in the cathedral garden.
➕ G7 ✉ 2 Werburgh Street ☎ 454 0306 🕐 Daily
🚌 Cross-city buses

LORD EDWARD (€€€)

www.lordedward.ie
Dublin's oldest seafood restaurant serves a range of excellent fish dishes, ranging from Galway Bay oysters to sole Véronique, in traditional surroundings.
➕ F7 ✉ 23 Christchurch Place ☎ 454 2420
🕐 Lunch Wed–Fri, dinner Wed–Sat 🚌 Cross-city buses

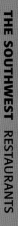

MEXICO TO ROME (€)

www.mexicotorome.com

A choice of menus allows you to mix Mexican with Italian, Irish and Asian dishes. A tapas menu is also available. It's popular and can be busy.

🛨 G7 ✉ 23 East Essex Street ☎ 677 2727
🕓 Lunch and dinner daily
🚆 Tara Street 🚌 Cross-city buses

MONGOLIAN BARBEQUE (€)

www.mongolianbbq.ie

Offers an unusual dining experience. Create your own dish at the buffet with Asian ingredients.

🛨 G7 ✉ 7 Anglesea Street ☎ 670 4154 🕓 Dinner Tue–Sun 🚌 Cross-city buses

MONTY'S OF KATMANDU (€€)

www.montys.ie

The city's only Nepalese restaurant, located in Temple Bar, offers intriguing South Asian dishes. It draws people from a wide area and is enhanced by the friendly staff.

🛨 G7 ✉ 28 Eustace Street ☎ 670 4911 🕓 Lunch, dinner Mon–Sat 🚆 Tara Street 🚌 Cross-city buses

ODESSA LOUNGE & GRILL (€€)

www.odessa.ie

This 1970s-inspired restaurant attracts a hip clientele. Popular for late Sunday brunch.

🛨 G7 ✉ 14 Dame Court ☎ 670 7634 🕓 Lunch,

dinner daily, brunch Sat–Sun
🚆 Pearse 🚌 Cross-city buses

PICHET (€€)

www.pichetrestaurant.ie

Classic wholesome bistro food with a modern twist by chefs formerly at the Michelin-starred L'Ecrivain (▷ 86). Good service and attention to detail.

🛨 H7 ✉ 14–15 Trinity Street ☎ 677 1060
🕓 Mon–Fri 8am–10.30pm, Sat noon–10, Sun 1–9
🚌 Cross-city buses

QUEEN OF TARTS (€)

www.queenoftarts.ie

Delicious cakes, bakes and tarts, all made on the premises, feature in this tiny traditional tea shop (bigger sister on nearby Cow's Lane). Unmissable.

🛨 G7 ✉ Cork Hill, Dame Street ☎ 670 7499 🕓 Daily 8.30–7 🚆 Tara Street
🚌 Cross-city buses

IN VOGUE

Dublin's reputation as a fashionable youth-orientated city is borne out by the capital's cosmopolitan restaurant scene. Listed on these pages are some of the city's most popular haunts. It is esssential to make reservations at the upscale and Michelin-starred restaurants. Even the trendiest places offer excellent value early-bird menus (before 7pm). If you want to linger, check your table's not booked for a second party.

THE SHACK (€€)

www.shackrestaurant.ie

A cosy Temple Bar restaurant offering Irish and European dishes made using the best fresh ingredients.

🛨 G7 ✉ 24 East Essex Street ☎ 679 0043
🕓 Lunch and dinner daily
🚆 Tara Street
🚌 Cross-city buses

THAI ORCHID (€€)

Spread over three floors, you will get all the established Thai specials here, well cooked and presented. Courteous Thai staff in traditional costume serve you, while Thai music plays in the background.

🛨 H6 ✉ 7 Westmoreland Street ☎ 671 9969
🕓 Lunch Mon–Sat, dinner daily 🚌 Cross-city buses

TRASTEVERE (€)

www.trastevere.ie

Upbeat eatery that blends authentic Italian dishes with a taste of New York.

🛨 G7 ✉ 1 Temple Bar Square ☎ 607 8343
🕓 Lunch and dinner Mon–Sat, Sun from 3.30pm 🚆 Tara Street 🚌 Cross-city buses

YAMAMORI (€€)

www.yamamorinoodles.ie

Japanese noodle and sushi house frequented by young Dubliners. Good choice of authentic dishes to suit all palates.

🛨 G7 ✉ 71–72 South Great George's Street ☎ 475 5001 🕓 Lunch and dinner daily 🚌 Cross-city buses

Run-down by the 1990s, the area north of the River Liffey has been undergoing a face-lift and the famous O'Connell Street and the shopping streets off it are all smartened up. The Docklands are developing rapidly.

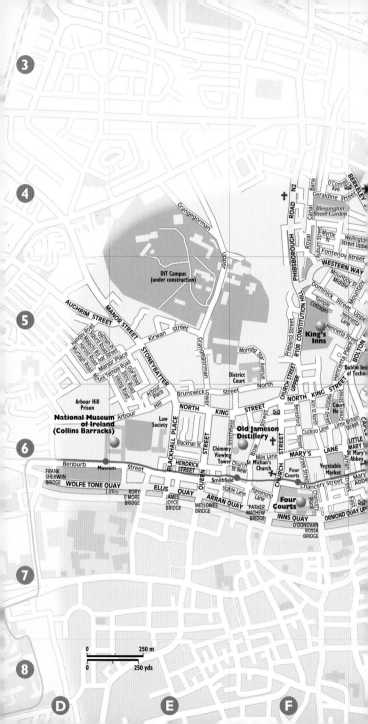

Collins Barracks

Collins Barracks contains the National Museum's collection of decorative arts

THE BASICS

www.museum.ie

+ E6
✉ Benburb Street
☎ 677 7444
🕐 Tue–Sat 10–5, Sun 2–5
🍴 Café
🚉 Heuston; Luas Museum
🚌 25, 25A, 66, 67, 90
♿ Very good
💷 Free
❓ Book tours in advance (inexpensive)

HIGHLIGHTS

● Old barracks building
● Fonthill vase
● Multistory clock
● 'The Way We Wore' exhibition
● Curator's Choice

Here you can view the decorative arts and social history collections of the National Museum—products of Irish artists and craftspeople that had been hidden from view for many years.

The building Sir Thomas Burgh (1670–1730), best known as architect of the Old Library in Trinity College (▷ 72–73), also designed Dublin's large Royal Barracks, just over a mile (1.6km) outside the city. Built in 1704, on high ground overlooking the River Liffey, they were handed over in 1922 to the Irish State, which named them after Michael Collins, the revolutionary leader killed in an ambush towards the end of the Civil War. Until decommissioning in 1988, they were generally thought to be the oldest military barracks still in use anywhere in the world.

Exhibits The barracks opened as an annex to the National Museum in 1997, greatly strengthening Dublin's cultural and historical focus. The items on display range from the 17th century right up to the present day and comprise Irish silver, glass and furniture, all of which reached a high point of artistic excellence particularly in the 18th century. Don't miss the Chinese porcelain Fonthill vase, which has managed to survive its well-documented wanderings in Asia and Europe, or the clock whose winding chains extend the height of two floors. Permanent exhibitions include 250 years of Irish clothing and jewelry, 'The Way We Wore', and a homage to the influential designer and architect Eileen Gray.

Studying at the Hugh Lane (left); The Punt by Jean-Baptiste-Camille Corot (right)

Degas, Monet, Corot and Renoir are among the Impressionist artists whose paintings are on display in this gallery that also looks back over 100 years of Irish art, including paintings and stained glass.

Philanthropist The Hugh Lane Gallery fills a niche between the old masters on display in the National Gallery (▷ 65) and the ultramodern creations in the Irish Museum of Modern Art (▷ 96) at Kilmainham. Built as a town house in 1763 by the Earl of Charlemont to the designs of Sir William Chambers, the gallery now bears the name of Sir Hugh Lane who drowned when the *Lusitania* sank in 1915. Before his death, Sir Hugh, who established Dublin's Municipal Gallery of Modern Art (a world first) in 1908, added a codicil to his will stating that a group of 39 of his Impressionist pictures, which were then in London, should go to Dublin. However, the codicil was unwitnessed, so London claimed the canvases and kept them until an agreement was reached in 1959 that the two cities would share them. The gallery has a programme of temporary exhibitions, including retrospectives of Irish art. You can visit the reconstructed studio of Francis Bacon, complete with its entire contents of more than 7,500 items.

Modern art Irish artists of the last hundred years, including Osborne, Yeats, Orpen, Bacon and Le Brocquy, are well represented, and modern European artists include Beuys and Albers. Make sure you see the stunning examples of stained glass by Clarke, Hone and Scanlon.

THE BASICS

www.hughlane.ie

🔢 G5

✉ Charlemont House, Parnell Square North

☎ 222 5550

🕐 Tue–Thu 10–6, Fri, Sat 10–5, Sun 11–5

🍴 Café

🚂 Connolly

🚌 Cross-city buses

♿ Good

♿ Free

HIGHLIGHTS

● Impressionist paintings
● Jack Yeats, *There is no Night*
● Orpen, *Homage to Manet*
● Stained glass by Harry Clarke
● Francis Bacon's studio
● Free concerts on Sunday Jun–Sep
● The Sean Scully Gallery

Dublin Writers Museum

TOP 25

The Gallery of Writers (left); modern stained-glass window (middle); children's room (right)

THE BASICS

www.writersmuseum.com

🚹 G5

✉ 18 Parnell Square North

☎ 872 2077

🕐 Mon–Sat 10–5, Sun and public hols 11–5

🍴 Café; Chapter One (▷ 60) restaurant in basement

🚇 Connolly

🚌 Cross-city buses

♿ Ground floor good (a few steps into the building)

💷 Moderate

❓ Excellent audio guide

HIGHLIGHTS

● Letters of Thomas Moore and Maria Edgeworth
● Yeats manuscript
● Indenture signed by Swift
● Painted ceiling and doors in the Gallery of Writers

For centuries a meeting point for gifted writers, Dublin has become the hub of a great literary tradition. This museum celebrates their diverse talents and displays a truly fascinating range of the writers' memorabilia.

Great Irish writers Many languages have been spoken by Ireland's inhabitants down the centuries, including Norse, Irish and Norman French, but it was with the establishment of English as the lingua franca in the 17th century that Dublin's literary reputation was established. Restoration dramatists such as George Farquhar were followed 50 years later by the brilliance and acerbic wit of Jonathan Swift. At the end of the 19th century, a new era dawned with the emergence of Oscar Wilde, whose epigrams enthralled the world. Around the turn of the 20th century, William Butler Yeats, encouraged by the flourishing Irish literary movement, helped found the Abbey Theatre, which opened in 1904. His contemporary, George Bernard Shaw, and subsequent Irish writers such as James Joyce, Samuel Beckett and Brendan Behan have continued to open new horizons in world literature.

Displays Photographs, paintings and other items linked with Ireland's literary titans are backed up with lots of explanatory material. First editions and rare volumes abound, and there are original letters of the poet Thomas Moore, a manuscript of W. B. Yeats and an indenture signed by Jonathan Swift. The house itself is spectacular.

You will find all things Joycean at the James Joyce Centre, especially on the murals

James Joyce Centre

Of all the literati to grace the Dublin scene during the 20th century, James Joyce has undoubtedly earned the greatest reputation internationally, so it is fitting that a whole house is devoted to the writer and his work.

Connections This beautifully restored 18th-century house, in an impressive street of Georgian redbrick residences just 275m (300yds) from O'Connell Street, is home to the James Joyce Centre. Initially, its Joycean connection was established through a dancing master called Denis J. Maginni, who leased one of the rooms in the house around the turn of the 20th century and appears as a character in *Ulysses*. Tours are available around the house and give the opportunity to listen to tapes of 'Uncle James', reading from *Ulysses* and *Finnegans Wake*.

Memorabilia Start your visit on the top floor where there's an atmospheric display of re-created period rooms, videos and computer installations, as well as a host of items relating to Joyce's life and work, including furniture from the Paris apartment where he worked on *Finnegans Wake*. Don't miss the front door out in the court-yard, rescued from the now demolished No. 7 Eccles Street, Leopold Bloom's address in *Ulysses*. The venue is a starting point for an 80–90 minute walking tour (payable separately) of Joycean sites on the north side of the city. You can buy a taped walking tour quite inexpensively in the shop and explore Joycean sights at your leisure.

THE BASICS

www.jamesjoyce.ie

🔲 H5

✉ 35 North Great George's Street

☎ 878 8547

🕐 Mon–Sat 10–5, Sun 12–5; closed Mon Oct–Mar

🍴 Café

🚆 Connolly

🚌 Cross-city buses

♿ Few

💰 Moderate

❓ Guided tours of house and Joycean Dublin

HIGHLIGHTS

● Joyce family members
● Recordings
● Library
● Portraits of characters in *Ulysses*
● No. 7 Eccles Street door

THE NORTH TOP 25

O'Connell Street

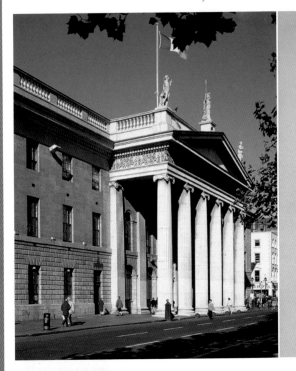

HIGHLIGHTS

- Portico decoration, statues and plaques on the General Post Office
- The Spire
- Clery's department store
- Eason bookshop
- Daniel O'Connell statue

An impressive, tree-lined thorough-fare leading down to the River Liffey, O'Connell Street has witnessed some memorable events in Irish history.

Grandiose monuments Two monuments dominate either end of O'Connell Street. Close to O'Connell Bridge is the mighty statue of Daniel O'Connell, passionate supporter of Catholic emancipation for Ireland. At the northern end is the monument to Charles Stewart Parnell, the leader of the struggle for Irish Home Rule.

General Post Office This building symbolizes the birthplace of modern Ireland. It was designed by Francis Johnston (1814–18), with statues by John Smith that dominate the skyline. Inside, the reading of the Proclamation of the Irish Republic

took place during the Easter Rising of 1916. The insurgents were forced to surrender after the interior was reduced to rubble (bullet chips on the portico columns are a reminder of the bitter struggle) and 16 were later executed. However, their stand led to the creation of modern Ireland and a salute is given here in their memory at the annual St. Patrick's Day parade. The museum on the ground floor houses the 'Letters, Lives and Liberty' exhibition, which gives an insight into the role of the Post Office in Irish society and includes a copy of the 1916 Proclamation.

Monument of Light Known as the Spire, this striking edifice was unveiled in 2003. Made of stainless steel and 120m (393ft) high, it stands on the site across the road from the General Post Office where Nelson's Column used to be.

The General Post Office (left) in O'Connell Street—scene of a major incident during the Easter Rising of 1916; detail from the statue and monument to Daniel O'Connell (right) on the street that bears his name

THE BASICS
General Post Office
✚ H5
✉ O'Connell Street
☎ 705 8833
⏱ Mon–Sat 8.30–6. Museum: 10–5
🚆 Tara Street
🚌 Cross-city buses; Luas Abbey Street
♿ Few
🎟 Free

53

More to See

CUSTOM HOUSE

Designed by James Gandon in 1791, the Custom House is an outstanding example of Georgian architecture and one of Dublin's finest buildings. Burned down by the IRA in 1921, it has been beautifully restored.

➕ J6 ✉ Custom House Quay ☎ 888 2538 ⏰ Mon–Fri 10–1, 2–4 🚉 Tara Street 🚌 Cross-city buses; Luas Busáras ♿ Good 💷 Inexpensive

DOCKLANDS

www.ddda.ie

The redevelopment of the former docks stretches from the Custom House east along the north of the Liffey to North Wall Quay, with massive developments on the south bank, too. They are linked by the Sean O' Casey Bridge (2005) and the Samuel Beckett Bridge (2010). Residential property, offices, cultural venues, shops, hotels and restaurants are changing the face of the city.

➕ J6–M6 ✉ North of the Liffey 🚉 Tara Street 🚌 Cross-city buses; Luas Connolly Station

FAMINE FIGURES

A series of emaciated figures along the quays commemorates the Great Famine of 1845–49. (The sculptor, Rowan Gillespie, is also behind the 'Spiderman' scaling the Treasury Building on Grand Canal Street.) Look for the World Poverty Stone nearby.

➕ J6 ✉ Custom House Quay 🚉 Tara Street 🚌 Cross-city buses; Luas Busáras

FOUR COURTS

Home to the Irish law courts since 1796, the Four Courts has much in common with the Custom House—primarily its designer, James Gandon. This Dublin landmark also suffered fire damage during the turbulent events of 1921. Visits are only permitted when courts are in session.

➕ F6 ✉ Inns Quay ☎ 888 6000 🚌 Cross-city buses; Luas Four Courts ♿ Few 💷 Free

GARDEN OF REMEMBRANCE

The statue of the *Children of Lír* is the focal point of this contemplative garden, dedicated to those who died

The statue Children of Lír

The copper dome of the Custom House

in pursuit of Irish independence. A poignant Irish fairy tale, about three children turned into swans by a wicked stepmother, inspired Oisín Kelly's bronze sculpture (1971).
✚ G5 ✉ Garden of Remembrance, Parnell Square East ☎ 821 3021 🚌 Cross-city buses

GRESHAM HOTEL
www.gresham-hotels-dublin.com
Once Dublin's grandest hotel (▷ 112), the Gresham is steeped in history. In the 1960s, the Beatles played an impromptu session here, the band's only live performance in Ireland, and the renowned traditional Irish band, the Chieftains, were formed here.
✚ H5 ✉ 23 Upper O'Connell Street ☎ 874 6881 🚌 Cross-city buses

KING'S INNS
www.kingsinns.ie
The honorable society of the King's Inns is the impressive setting for Dublin law students training for the bar. Steeped in tradition, this beautiful building was begun by James Gandon.
✚ F5 ✉ Henrietta Street 🕐 View from outside only 🚌 83

OLD JAMESON DISTILLERY
www.jamesonwhiskey.com
Explore the history of Irish whiskey-making through exhibits and audio-visual presentations on the site of the old Jameson Distillery. Sample a drop at the visitor bar—included in the ticket. Guided tours only.
✚ F6 ✉ Bow Street, Smithfield ☎ 807 2355 🕐 Daily 9–6. Tours every 40 min; last tour 5.30 🍴 🚌 68, 69, 79, 90; Luas Smithfield ♿ Good 💷 Expensive

ST. MARY'S PRO CATHEDRAL
www.procathedral.ie
Mother church for Catholic Dublin, affectionately known as 'the Pro', this impressive 1825 building has hosted many Church and State occasions.
✚ H5 ✉ Marlborough Street ☎ 874 5441 🕐 Mon–Fri 7.30–6.45, Sat 7.30–7.15, Sun 9–1.45, 5.30–7.45, public hols 10–1.30 🚌 Cross-city buses; Luas Abbey Street

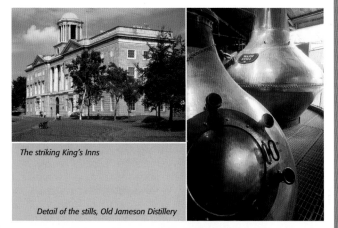

The striking King's Inns

Detail of the stills, Old Jameson Distillery

A Walk North of the River

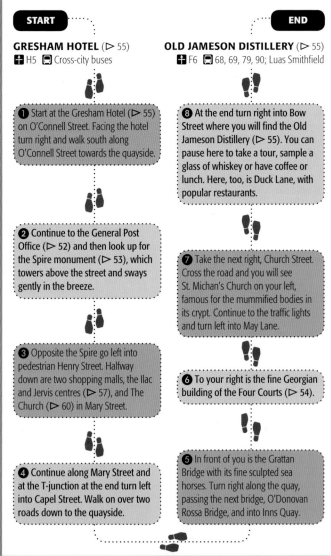

This walk is in the lesser-known northern district of Dublin, undergoing a major rejuvenation. It also takes in part of the quays.

DISTANCE: 2km (1.25 miles) **ALLOW:** 1 hour plus stops

START

GRESHAM HOTEL (▷ 55)
H5   Cross-city buses

END

OLD JAMESON DISTILLERY (▷ 55)
F6   68, 69, 79, 90; Luas Smithfield

① Start at the Gresham Hotel (▷ 55) on O'Connell Street. Facing the hotel turn right and walk south along O'Connell Street towards the quayside.

② Continue to the General Post Office (▷ 52) and then look up for the Spire monument (▷ 53), which towers above the street and sways gently in the breeze.

③ Opposite the Spire go left into pedestrian Henry Street. Halfway down are two shopping malls, the Ilac and Jervis centres (▷ 57), and The Church (▷ 60) in Mary Street.

④ Continue along Mary Street and at the T-junction at the end turn left into Capel Street. Walk on over two roads down to the quayside.

⑧ At the end turn right into Bow Street where you will find the Old Jameson Distillery (▷ 55). You can pause here to take a tour, sample a glass of whiskey or have coffee or lunch. Here, too, is Duck Lane, with popular restaurants.

⑦ Take the next right, Church Street. Cross the road and you will see St. Michan's Church on your left, famous for the mummified bodies in its crypt. Continue to the traffic lights and turn left into May Lane.

⑥ To your right is the fine Georgian building of the Four Courts (▷ 54).

⑤ In front of you is the Grattan Bridge with its fine sculpted sea horses. Turn right along the quay, passing the next bridge, O'Donovan Rossa Bridge, and into Inns Quay.

Shopping

ARNOTTS
www.arnotts.ie
Arnotts, Ireland's largest department store, stocks everything fashionable in clothes, interiors, household, leisure, entertainment and cosmetics.
➕ G6 ✉ 12 Henry Street ☎ 805 0400 🚇 Connolly 🚌 Cross-city buses; Luas Jervis

THE CHQ BUILDING
www.chq.ie
A 19th-century wine and tobacco store has been transformed into a mall of smart boutiques, shops, coffee bars and Mitchell & Sons, Dublin's oldest fine wine merchants.
➕ J6 ✉ IFSC, George's Dock ☎ No phone 🚇 Tara Street 🚌 Cross-city buses; Luas Busáras

CLERYS
www.clerys.ie
A Dublin institution. Many romantic assignations have been made beneath the clock outside this department store, which opened in 1853.
➕ H6 ✉ Lower O'Connell Street ☎ 878 6000 🚇 Tara Street 🚌 Cross-city buses

DUBLIN WRITERS MUSEUM BOOKSHOP
www.writersmuseum.com
This excellent shop, in the home of literary Dublin, covers all aspects of Irish writing from travel to poetry, including works by many of the writers featured in the museum.
➕ G5 ✉ 18 Parnell Street North ☎ 872 2077 🚇 Connolly 🚌 Cross-city buses

EASON
www.eason.ie
This vast bookstore has a huge selection of books and magazines together with stationery, art equipment and music. Café. Several branches, including one near Trinity College.
➕ H6 ✉ 40 Lower O'Connell Street ☎ 858 3800 🚇 Tara Street or Connolly 🚌 Cross-city buses

ILAC CENTRE
www.ilac.ie
Dublin's longest established shopping mall has had a face-lift. Among the labyrinth of smaller shops and high street names are branches of Dunnes and Debenhams department stores.
➕ G6 ✉ Henry Street ☎ 828 8900 🚇 Tara Street 🚌 Cross-city buses; Luas Jervis

JERVIS CENTRE
www.jervis.ie
Popular with Dubliners, this modern mall is spread over two floors and four mezzanines. It has more than 60 shops, a food court and regular events and family days.
➕ G6 ✉ 125 Abbey Street Upper ☎ 878 1323 🚇 Tara Street 🚌 Cross-city buses; Luas Jervis

MOORE STREET MALL
www.moorestmall.com
Multicultural shopping plus an enticing food market displaying organic and exotic ingredients from around the globe.
➕ G5 ✉ 58–66 Parnell Street ☎ 873 3416 🚇 Connolly 🚌 Cross-city buses; Luas Middle Abbey Street

PENNEY'S
www.primark.ie
Part of the popular Primark group, with low-cost clothing for men, women and kids.
➕ H6 ✉ O'Connell Street, nr junction with Prince's Street ☎ 656 6666 🚌 Cross-city buses; Luas Abbey Street

WINDING STAIR
www.winding-stair.com
A literary landmark overlooking Ha'penny Bridge, this atmospheric bookshop offers a wide range of new and second-hand books. Delightful first floor restaurant.
➕ G6 ✉ 40 Lower Ormond Quay ☎ 872 6576 🚇 Tara Street 🚌 Cross-city buses

Entertainment and Nightlife

ABBEY

www.abbeytheatre.ie

Founded in 1904, the national theater played a vital role in the renaissance of Irish culture in the late 19th century. The quality of the performances and playwriting is rarely surpassed. Many first runs go to New York's Broadway or London's West End.

➕ H6 ✉ 26 Abbey Street Lower ☎ 878 7222 🚇 Connolly/Tara Street 🚌 Cross-city buses

CINEWORLD

www.cineworld.ie

Multiplex with 17 screens showing the latest releases and blockbusters.

➕ G6 ✉ Parnell Centre, Parnell Street ☎ 1520 880 444 🚇 Connolly 🚌 Cross-city buses

GATE

www.gate-theatre.ie

Some of Dublin's most inspired and sophisticated plays, performed in an 18th-century building. The theater's actors, playwrights and productions have an international reputation and tour the world.

➕ G5 ✉ Cavendish Row, Parnell Square ☎ 874 4045 🚇 Connolly 🚌 Cross-city buses

LAUGHTER LOUNGE

www.laughterlounge.com

Treat yourself to a good giggle with a host of local international stand-up talent staged on Thursday, Friday and Saturday.

➕ H6 ✉ 4–8 Eden Quay ☎ 878 3003 🚇 Tara Street 🚌 Cross-city buses

GRAND CENTRAL

www.louisfitzgerald.com

Converted from a 19th-century banking hall. Beers on tap, wines and lunchtime menu.

➕ H6 ✉ 10–11 O'Connell Street ☎ 872 8658 🚌 Cross-city buses; Luas Abbey Street

THE O2

www.theo2.ie

A state-of-the-art entertainment venue in Docklands. Top names in music and comedy appear, plus musicals, opera and concerts. It is Dublin's star-studded attraction, and tickets sell fast.

DANCE

When looking for the best dance clubs in Dublin, go by the name of that particular night at the club rather than the name of the venue itself. Most good dance nights are independently run gigs organized by promoters and staged in different places around town. *The Event Guide,* distributed free in bars and cafés around the city, has the most comprehensive and accurate listings. The Tourist Information Office will also help you find your best venue.

➕ M6 ✉ North Wall Quay ☎ 819 8888 🚌 151; Luas Docklands Station

PEACOCK

www.abbeytheatre.ie

In the same complex as the Abbey, its younger sibling is a platform for emerging Irish talent.

➕ H6 ✉ 26 Abbey Street Lower ☎ 878 7222 🚇 Connolly/Tara Street 🚌 Cross-city buses

QUAY 14

www.morrisonhotel.ie

This is a stylish, top celeb-spotting venue in the Morrison Hotel, where the beautiful people hang out.

➕ G6 ✉ Ormond Quay Lower ☎ 887 2400 🚌 Cross-city buses

RYAN'S

http://ryans.fxbuckley.ie

Landmark 19th-century pub filled with original mahogany snugs, etched mirrors and gas lamps. Past drinkers include American presidents Bush Sr. and Jr., plus JFK. Full gastro bar menu specializing in steak.

➕ D6 ✉ 28 Parkgate Street ☎ 677 6097 🚌 Cross-city buses; Luas Museum

SAVOY

www.savoy.ie

Now owned by the IMC group, the cinema has six screens. It bows to modernity while retaining its historic interior.

➕ H5 ✉ O'Connell Street ☎ 0818 221122 🚇 Connolly 🚌 Cross-city buses

Restaurants

PRICES

Prices are approximate, based on a 3-course meal for one person.

€€€	over €40
€€	€25–€40
€	under €25

BESHOFF'S (€)

www.beshoffrestaurant.ie
Great fish and chips with catch-of-the-day specials at this Dublin institution. Grab a window seat for views of busy O'Connell Street.
🚇 H6 ✉ 6 Upper O'Connell Street ☎ 872 4400 🕐 Daily 12–12 🚉 Connolly 🚌 Cross-city buses; Luas Abbey Street

CHAPTER ONE (€€€)

www.chapteronerestaurant.com
One of Dublin's most elegant restaurants nestles within the basement of the Dublin Writers Museum. Irish contemporary food, with a nod to French classic cooking, is on offer. Good wine vault.
🚇 G5 ✉ 18–19 Parnell Square ☎ 873 2266 🕐 Lunch Tue–Fri, dinner Tue–Sat 🚉 Connolly 🚌 Cross-city buses

THE CHURCH (€–€€€)

www.thechurch.ie
The setting is spectacular. The galleried former St. Mary's Church boasts a mezzanine area for smart dining; a downstairs bar serving light meals, and a café. There is also an outside terrace and a basement club and bar. Very popular.
🚇 G6 ✉ Mary Street ☎ 828 0102 🕐 Lunch, dinner daily 🚌 Luas Jervis

COBALT CAFÉ (€)

Airy café with artworks on the walls. Tasty sandwiches and cakes.
🚇 H5 ✉ 16 North Great George's Street ☎ 873 0313 🕐 Mon–Sat 10–6 🚉 Connolly 🚌 Cross-city buses

IL FORNAIO (€–€€)

www.ilfornaio.ie
Authentic Italian food here and friendly Italian service to match. Pizza, pasta and classic desserts.
🚇 J6 ✉ 1B Valentia House, Custom House Square, IFSC ☎ 672 1853 🕐 Daily 🚉 Connolly 🚌 Luas Busáras

HARBOURMASTER BAR & RESTAURANT (€€)

www.harbourmaster.ie
Located in the old Dock Offices in the heart of the growing financial Docklands district, with a waterside setting. There is an old-style pub and a modern dining room serving wholesome food, ranging from pan-fried scallops to rump of lamb.
🚇 J6 ✉ Custom House Dock ☎ 670 1688 🕐 Lunch, dinner daily 🚉 Connolly 🚌 Luas Busáras

MV CILL AIRNE (€€)

www.mvcillairne.com
Historic little ship moored in Docklands with a good restaurant, bistro and bar. Convenient for the O2.
🚇 K6 ✉ Quay 16, North Wall Quay ☎ 817 8760 🕐 Daily lunch and dinner 🚉 Docklands Station 🚌 Luas Busáras

OLD JAMESON DISTILLERY (€€)

Enjoy tasty, down-to-earth Irish dishes in the 3rd Still Restaurant, including fish and chips, on the site of the distillery.
🚇 F6 ✉ Smithfield Village ☎ 807 2355 🕐 Daily 10–5 🚌 83; Luas Smithfield

PANEM (€)

Excellent little bakery with a tiny café where you watch the bakers conjure up croissants, focaccias and sweet treats. Try the delicious special hot chocolate.
🚇 G6 ✉ Ha'penny Bridge House, 21 Lower Ormond Quay ☎ 872 8510 🕐 Mon–Fri 8–6, Sat 9–6, Sun 10–4.30 🚌 Luas Jervis

A GOOD CATCH

Fresh fish is plentiful in Dublin restaurants. Oysters, mussels, crab, prawns (shrimps), salmon, ray, mackerel, sole, whiting and trout are all found in local waters. For a truly Irish gastronomic experience, wash down a dozen fresh oysters with a glass of Guinness and mop up the salty juices with home-baked brown bread.

This district, south of the River Liffey, has been Dublin's most elegant and fashionable area since the 18th century. Here you will find Trinity College, the national museums and elegant Georgian squares.

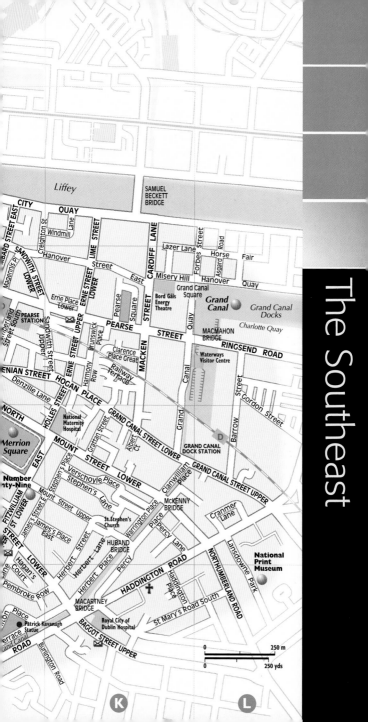

Liffey

CITY QUAY

SAMUEL BECKETT BRIDGE

St Windmill Lane

Hanover Street

Lime Street

Cardiff Lane

Lazer Lane

Forbes Street

Horse Road

Asgard

Fair

Magennis

Sandwith Street Lower

Erne Street Lower

Erne Place Lower

Pearse Square

Macken Street

Misery Hill

Hanover Quay

Grand Canal Square

Bord Gáis Energy Theatre

Grand Canal

Grand Canal Docks

Charlotte Quay

PEARSE STATION

Sandwith Street Upper

Sandwith Street South

Cumberland Street South

Brunswick Place

PEARSE STREET

Quay

MACMAHON BRIDGE

MACMAHON BRIDGE

RINGSEND ROAD

ENIAN STREET

Denzille Lane

HOGAN PLACE

Erne Street Upper

Holles Street

Clarence Place Great

Harmony Row

Railway Terrace

Canal

Grand Canal

Waterways Visitor Centre

St Gordon Street

NORTH

Merrion Square

MOUNT STREET LOWER

National Maternity Hospital

GRAND CANAL STREET LOWER

Grattan Street

Albert Ct

Clanwilliam Place

GRAND CANAL STREET UPPER

Barrow

GRAND CANAL DOCK STATION

Number nty-Nine

EAST

FITZWILLIAM

ST LOWER

Verschoyle Place

Stephen's Place

Stephen's Lane

Mount Street Upper

James's Street East

James's Place East

St.Stephen's Church

Warrington Place

McKenny Place

Percy Lane

MCKENNY BRIDGE

Cranmer Lane

Lansdowne Park

National Print Museum

STREET

Hogan's Court

Pembroke Row

Herbert Street

Herbert Lane

Herbert Place

HUBAND BRIDGE

Percy

HADDINGTON ROAD

NORTHUMBERLAND ROAD

Haddington Place

St Mary's Road South

ROAD SOUTH

Place

Patrick Kavanagh Statue

errace and Canal

ROAD

Burlington Road

MACARTNEY BRIDGE

BAGGOT STREET UPPER

Royal City of Dublin Hospital

0   250 m
0   250 yds

K   L

The Southeast

Grand Canal

A peaceful scene by the Grand Canal (left); Viking Splash at Grand Canal Quay (right)

THE BASICS

🟩 L7 (Grand Canal Docks)
🍴 Several cafés and restaurants
🚇 Grand Canal Dock
🚌 2, 3

HIGHLIGHTS

● Peaceful strolls along the canal
● Grand Canal Square
● Waterways Visitor Centre
● River cruise and floating restaurant La Peniche (▷ 87)

Here the city's tranquil calm meets its exciting future in the regeneration of the Grand Canal area, the new cultural and commercial focal point of Dublin.

Early days Crossing Leinster from Dublin to the River Shannon in Offaly, the Grand Canal forms a 6km (4-mile) loop around Dublin. In the 18th century the canal provided an important means of transportation but there has been no commercial traffic on the water since the early 1960s. It's now a haven for wildlife, and you can take a boat trip down the canal, or the two-hour walk all the way to Kilmainham, stopping to rest and watch the swans slip by with the bronze of poet Patrick Kavanagh (1905–67), who loved this piece of leafy calm.

Looking to the future The huge 10,000sq m (107,639sq ft) piazza, opened in 2007 at Grand Canal Dock, is a hub of activity. Surrounded by tinted-glass office buildings, a five-star hotel, shops, cafés and restaurants and the diamond shaped Grand Canal Theatre (officially known as the Bord Gáis Energy Theatre), it has revitalized an almost forgotten area of Dublin. Striking red-glass paving covered with glowing light sticks and green polygon-shape planters, illuminate the square.

Waterways Visitor Centre Known to locals as 'the box in the docks', the modern white cube in the middle of the Grand Canal basin houses a visitor center, which traces the story of Ireland's inland waterways, their historical background and how they are used today.

Views of the imposing National Gallery fronted by its founder, William Dargan

The National Gallery enjoys considerable standing on the international scene as the home of one of Europe's premier collections of old masters.

Origins Facing onto Merrion Square, the National Gallery is set in relaxing green surroundings. The gallery was established in 1854 and opened in 1864 to display old master paintings to inspire budding Irish artists of the mid-Victorian period. Its contents have expanded 20-fold in the century-and-a-half since then, helped by many bequests. These include works by Vermeer, Velázquez and Murillo; the legacy of one-third of George Bernard Shaw's residual estate enabled the gallery to acquire important works by Fragonard and J. L. David, among others.

Masterpieces The Irish paintings, on the ground floor, show a progression from the 18th century onward while the old masters, for which the gallery is famous, are on the next floor. Wide coverage is given to most European schools of painting—including icons, early Italians (Uccello and Fra Angelico), Renaissance (Titian, Tintoretto), Dutch and Flemish (Rembrandt, Rubens), Spanish (Goya), French (Poussin) and British (Reynolds and Raeburn, among others). The display also covers Impressionists and modern painters up to Picasso. One room is devoted to watercolors and drawings—including 31 by Turner, shown every January. The Millennium Wing, opened in 2002, houses an area for the study of Irish art and temporary exhibition galleries.

HIGHLIGHTS

- Yeats Archive
- Fra Angelico, *Attempted Martyrdom of SS Cosmas and Damian*
- Titian, *Ecce Homo*
- Vermeer, *A Lady Writing*
- Rembrandt, *Rest on the Flight into Egypt*
- Van Gogh, *Rooftops in Paris*
- Picasso, *Still Life with a Mandolin*
- Millennium Wing

THE SOUTHEAST TOP 25

National Museum

The National Museum houses most of Ireland's greatest archaeological treasures. A visit here is a must for a deeper understanding of the country's prehistoric history and culture.

Extensive collections For more than a century, the twin institutions of the National Museum (1890) and the National Library have faced each other across the square leading to the Dáil, or Houses of Parliament. On the ground floor, the museum displays western Europe's most extensive collection of prehistoric gold ornaments, mostly dating from the Bronze Age (c1500–500BC). The torcs and jewelry are stunning, as are the brooches, crosses and croziers (AD600–1200), from Ireland's early Christian monasteries, on show in the Treasury. Among the greatest gems in this

In an attractive leafy location, the National Museum is a wonderful showcase for Ireland's treasures (left); the beautiful galleried exhibition room of the National Museum features some of the most spectacular prehistoric gold ornaments of the collection (right)

dazzling collection are the eighth-century Tara Brooch, the Ardagh Chalice and the Derrynaflan Hoard. Don't miss the rare Tully Lough Cross, an Irish altar cross of the eighth or ninth century. Discovered in Roscommon in fragments, it has been meticulously reconstructed. The discovery of two Iron Age bog bodies in 2003 led to a radical new theory that linked them with sovereignty rituals as the 'Kingship and Sacrifice' exhibition explains.

History Upstairs, 'Viking Ireland' spans AD795–1170. It documents invasions, trades and crafts and has scale models of Viking Dublin. 'Medieval Ireland' covers life from the 12th century Anglo-Norman invasion to the Reformation. Further exhibitions display ceramics and glass from Ancient Cyprus and artefacts portraying life, death and religion in Ancient Egypt.

THE BASICS

www.museum.ie
☩ H8
✉ Kildare Street
☎ 677 7444
🕐 Tue–Sat 10–5, Sun 2–5
🍴 Café
🚉 Pearse
🚌 Cross-city buses; Luas St. Stephen's Green
♿ Ground floor good
🎟 Free
❓ Shop. Guided tours 45 minutes, small charge

Natural History Museum

Sketching a fiberglass hippo (left); old bones in a Victorian setting (right)

THE BASICS

www.museum.ie

⊞ J8

✉ Merrion Street

☎ 677 7444

🕐 Tue–Sat 10–5, Sun 2–5

🚉 Pearse

🚌 Cross-city buses

♿ Ground floor access only

🎟 Free

HIGHLIGHTS

- Giant Irish elk
- Great Irish wolfhound
- Fin whale
- Dodo skeleton
- Hummingbirds
- Small meteorite

Dubbed by locals as 'the dead zoo', the museum's old glass cases and creaking floorboards have changed little since its inauguration in 1857, when Dr. David Livingstone gave the first lecture on his 'African discoveries'.

Fauna The Natural History Museum is one of the four great national institutions flanking the Irish Houses of Parliament. The nucleus of its collection was assembled by the Royal Dublin Society long before it opened, and it has benefited greatly from subsequent gifts. Facing you as you enter is the skeleton of the giant Irish deer, better known as the Irish elk, with its impressive antlers. Beyond is a great array of Irish furred and feathered animals as well as an interesting collection of marine species.

Dodo The upper floor is given over to animals of the world, among them the great Irish wolfhound and a massive 20m-long (66ft) whale suspended from the ceiling. There is also a skeleton of a dodo and a cluster of hummingbirds. Geology is something of a sideline but is represented by a meteorite that landed in 1810 on County Tipperary in central Ireland. A different kind of curiosity is the outfit worn by Surgeon-Major Thomas Heazle Parke (1858–93), of the Royal Army Medical Corps, who became the first Irishman to cross Africa from coast to coast. A statue of him stands in front of the museum. The interactive Discovery Zone, divided into Life on Land and The Life Aquatic, is great for children.

Number Twenty Nine

The elegance of a bygone age in the Georgian Number Twenty Nine

So many of Dublin's 18th-century houses are used as offices that it is a pleasure to see this rare example, perfectly restored and sumptuously furnished in elegant period style.

The setting Merrion Square epitomizes the graciousness of Georgian Dublin. Three of its four sides are surrounded by four-floor red-brick houses, each elegant doorway crowned by a handsome fanlight. The view from the south side toward St. Stephen's (also known as the Pepper Canister for the shape of its cupola) is one of the city's most attractive streetscapes, and on the southeast corner of the square stands Number Twenty Nine, the only structure in Dublin to preserve the graceful middle-class domesticity of the 18th century.

Nostalgia You enter, as servants did, through the basement, passing the kitchen and pantry (that still has its ingenious rat-proof shelving) to reach the main living quarters on the ground level and parlor floor. Here you will find tasteful Georgian furniture and furnishings, paintings and costumes of the period 1780–1820. The small details are captivating—the hastener (tea trolley) in the kitchen, the feather shaving brush in the gentleman's washing room and the early exercise machine in the bedroom. Climb to the top floor to see the children's playroom, and on the way up admire the wood carving of Napoleon by Bozzanigo Torino in the master bedroom. Don't miss the exquisite Waterford crystal chandelier and the fine Mount Mellick embroidery.

THE BASICS

www.esb.
ie.numbertwentynine/

➕ J8

✉ 29 Fitzwilliam Street Lower

☎ 702 6165

🕐 Mid-Feb to mid-Dec Tue–Sat 10–5, Sun 12–5

🍴 Tea room

🚉 Pearse

🚍 7, 10, 45

♿ None

💷 Moderate

❓ Tours daily 3pm

HIGHLIGHTS

● Wood carving of Napoleon
● Examples of Mount Mellick embroidery
● Playroom
● Waterford crystal chandelier

St. Stephen's Green

TOP
25

HIGHLIGHTS

Newman House
● Apollo Room
● Upper floor Saloon
● Staircase
● Gerard Manley Hopkins' room

Newman University Church
● Marble panels
● Carved birds on capitals
● Ceiling
● Golden apse

A popular place when the sun comes out, this park was originally common land used for public hangings, among other activities. Among notable buildings around the green are Newman House and the Newman University Church.

A public garden By 1880, St. Stephen's Green had become a public garden, thanks to the benevolence of Lord Ardilaun, a member of the Guinness family. Don't miss the monuments and statues, or the lunchtime concerts in summer.

Newman House Newman House is actually two great houses. No. 85 was built in 1738; its walls and ceilings were decorated with stucco ornament by the Lafranchini brothers. Their most notable achievements are the figures of Apollo

Clockwise from top left: Plasterwork by the talented Lafranchini brothers in the Apollo Room, Newman House, St. Stephen's Green; the Saloon in Newman House; St. Stephen's Green in full bloom; fountain on St. Stephen's Green; enjoying the view

and the nine muses on the ground floor, and the extravagant ceiling of the Saloon. No. 85 was then bought by Richard Chapel Whaley who went on to build No. 86, embellishing it with fine stucco work. Great liberal intellectual, Cardinal John Henry Newman used the house in the 1850s, and subsequently it was used by literary greats Gerard Manley Hopkins and James Joyce.

Newman University Church This ornate, Byzantine-style church was built by Cardinal Newman on land between No. 86 and No. 87 to promote his ideals.

Fusiliers' Arch The monument (also known as Traitors' Arch) on the northwest corner of St. Stephen's Green is a tribute to soldiers of the Royal Dublin Fusiliers killed during the Boer War.

Trinity College

- *Book of Kells*
- *Book of Durrow*
- *Book of Armagh*
- Science Gallery

TIPS

- Everyone wants to see the *Book of Kells* and the best thing is to visit early or come out of season.
- A walking tour in the summer is an informative way to learn more about the college. Ask at the porter's lodge for information.

Stroll around the grounds of the famous college and visit the library, where you will find one of the most joyously decorative manuscripts of the first Christian millennium, the *Book of Kells*.

Surroundings An oasis of fresh air, Trinity College is also the noblest assemblage of classical buildings in the city. Inside, the open square is surrounded on three sides by some of Dublin's finest buildings—Paul Koralek's New Library (1978) to the south, Benjamin Woodward's splendidly carved Museum building (1853–55) to the east and Thomas Burgh's Old Library (1712–32) to the west. In 1857, Woodward altered Burgh's building and made its barrel-vaulted upper floor into a breathtaking space lined with books from floor to ceiling.

Clockwise from top left: Trinity College, synonymous with learning in Dublin; Trinity College's famous Old Library, housing Ireland's largest collection of books and the Book of Kells; Fellow's Square, with the Old Library in the background; Sphere within Sphere (1982–83) by Arnaldo Pomodoro, in the grounds of the college

Book of Kells The library is an appropriate setting for Ireland's greatest collection of medieval manuscripts. Among these, pride of place goes to the *Book of Kells* (*c*800), a Gospel book that has been bound in four separate sections so that its brilliantly ornamented pages and text may be viewed side by side. Displayed alongside are the important books of Durrow (*c*700) and Armagh (*c*800), the latter giving us most of the information we have about Ireland's patron saint, Patrick. The *Book of Kells* 'Turning Darkness into Light' exhibition has excellent displays telling the history of illuminated manuscripts and books. The exit is through the amazing Long Room library.

Science Gallery Opened in 2008, this gallery stages changing exhibitions which focus on the world of design, discovery and science.

THE BASICS

www.tcd.ie

H7

College Green

896 1000

Old Library Mon–Sat 9.30–5, Sun 9.30–4.30 (Oct–end Apr Sun 12–4.30). Campus daily

Pearse, Tara Street

Cross-city buses

Good

Campus free; Library and *Book of Kells* expensive

College tours May–end Nov

More to See

DOUGLAS HYDE GALLERY

www.douglashydegallery.com

Contemporary gallery providing talent from Ireland and overseas.

🔲 H7 ✉ Trinity College, Nassau Street entrance ☎ 608 1116 🕐 Mon–Fri 11–6, Thu 11–7, Sat 11–4.45 🚆 Pearse 🚌 Cross-city buses 🚾 Few 🖐 Free

GAIETY THEATRE

www.gaietytheatre.ie

Known as 'The Grand Old Lady of South King Street', this attractive venue, with its landmark Venetian facade, opened on 27 November 1871 with Sir Oliver Goldsmith's *She Stoops to Conquer* followed by burlesque, setting the scene for a continuing agenda of high-quality entertainment (▷ 82).

🔲 H8 ✉ King Street South ☎ 456 9569 🚆 Pearse 🚌 Cross-city buses; Luas St. Stephen's Green

IVEAGH GARDENS

One of Dublin's finest, yet least-known parks, was designed by Ninian Niven in 1865. The secluded gardens shelter a grotto, fountains, maze, sunken lawns, rockeries, wilderness and wood-lands. Exotic tree ferns and pre-1860s rose varieties in the Victorian Rosarium add to its romance.

🔲 H9 ✉ Clonmel Street ☎ 475 7816 🕐 Mon–Sat 8–6, Sun 10–6; closes at dusk in winter 🚌 Cross-city buses; Luas Harcourt 🖐 Free

LEINSTER HOUSE

www.oireachtas.ie

Leinster House is the seat of Irish government and home to Dáil Éireann (House of Representatives) and Senead Éireann (Senate). You can visit by prior arrangement when parliament is not in session.

🔲 J8 ✉ Kildare Street ☎ 618 3781 🚆 Pearse 🚌 Cross-city buses; Luas St. Stephen's Green 🚾 Good 🖐 Free

THE LITTLE MUSEUM OF DUBLIN

www.littlemuseum.ie

On the first floor of a Georgian building, this museum tells the

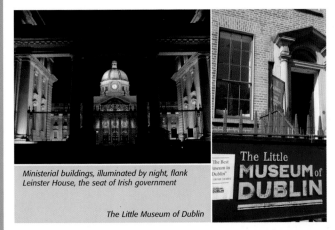

Ministerial buildings, illuminated by night, flank Leinster House, the seat of Irish government

The Little Museum of Dublin

story of 20th-century Dublin. Its collection of 5,000 artefacts is a result of a public appeal for historic objects and includes items from the 1913 Lockout, the 1960s women's movement and Gaelic Athletic Association (GAA) of the 1970s.

✚ H8 ✉ 15 St. Stephen's Green ◷ Daily 9.30–5, Thu 9.30–8 ☎ 661 1000 🚌 Cross-city buses; Luas St. Stephen's Green

MANSION HOUSE

The Mansion House has been the Lord Mayor of Dublin's official residence since 1715. In 1919 the first parliament of the Irish people met here to adopt Ireland's Declaration of Independence from Britain. The majestic Round Room is closed to visitors.

✚ H8 ✉ Dawson Street 🚉 Pearse
🍴 Fire (▷ 86) 🚌 Cross-city buses; Luas St. Stephen's Green

MERRION SQUARE

The best-preserved Georgian square in Dublin was home to Daniel O'Connell and William Butler Yeats,

among others. The public park is a hidden gem: take a look after a visit to Number Twenty Nine (▷ 69).

✚ J8 🚉 Pearse 🚌 Cross-city buses 👆 Free

MOLLY MALONE STATUE

The eponymous fishmonger of song is believed to have lived and worked in Dublin until her death in 1734.

✚ H7 ✉ Lower Grafton Street 🚉 Pearse
🚌 Cross-city buses

NATIONAL LIBRARY

www.nli.ie

The library houses the world's largest collection of Irish documentary material, comprising books, newspapers, manuscripts, drawings, maps and photographs. Research has to take place in the reading room. Most popular are the Genealogy Service and family history research departments. Excellent exhibitions.

✚ J7 ✉ Kildare Street ☎ 603 0213
◷ Mon–Wed 9.30–7.45, Thu–Fri 9.30–5, Sat 9.30–1 🍴 Café 🚉 Pearse 🚌 Cross-city buses; Luas St. Stephen's Green ♿ Good
👆 Free; reader's ticket required for info

Molly Malone statue by Jeanne Rynhart in Lower Grafton Street

Dublin City Arms

NATIONAL PRINT MUSEUM

www.nationalprintmuseum.ie

A little off the beaten track, but worth a visit. The old chapel houses objects related to the printing industry, with working machinery on display. Guided tours by retired printers bring it to life.

🕂 L9 ✉ Garrison Chapel, Beggar's Bush, Haddington Road ☎ 660 3770 🕔 Mon–Fri 9–5, Sat–Sun 2–5 🚃 Grand Canal Dock 🚌 7, 45, 63 ♿ Good, ground floor only ✋ Inexpensive

OSCAR WILDE'S HOUSE

www.amcd.ie

On the north side of Merrion Square is the house where Oscar Wilde lived from 1855 to 1876, now the American College Dublin. It was the first house to be built in the square in 1762 and is an excellent example of Georgian architecture.

🕂 J7 ✉ 1 Merrion Square 🚃 Pearse 🚌 Cross-city buses; Luas St. Stephen's Green ♿ No disabled access ❓ Not open to the public—view from the outside only

Royal College of Surgeons

OSCAR WILDE STATUE

Danny Osborne's life-size sculpture of Wilde, at the northwest corner of Merrion Square, was unveiled in 1997 and depicts the writer, lying languidly on a huge piece of granite. It is created from naturally-coloured Irish stone. The statue is especially haunting at night.

🕂 J7 ✉ Merrion Square 🚃 Pearse 🚌 Cross-city buses

ROYAL COLLEGE OF SURGEONS

One of Dublin's later Georgian constructions, this jewel of a building on the northwest corner of St. Stephen's Green dates from 1806 and was designed by architect Edward Parke.

🕂 H8 ✉ 123 St. Stephen's Green ☎ 402 2100 🚌 Cross-city buses; Luas St. Stephen's Green ♿ Few ✋ Free

ST. ANN'S CHURCH

www.stann.dublin.anglican.org

Patronized by influential residents of Georgian Dublin, this 1720 church has a stunning neo-Romanesque facade. Look for the Bread Shelf, part of a 300-year-old tradition. It also holds a number of concerts.

🕂 H7 ✉ Dawson Street ☎ 676 7727 🕔 Mon–Fri 10–4 and Sunday service 🚃 Pearse 🚌 Cross-city buses ♿ Good ✋ Free

VIKING SPLASH TOURS

www.vikingsplash.ie

Drive through Viking Dublin on amphibious buses before driving into the Grand Canal to finish the tour on water. Great fun.

🕂 H8 ✉ St. Stephen's Green ☎ 707 6000 🕔 Feb to mid-Nov regular daily tours depart from St. Stephen's Green (tours 90 minutes) ✋ Expensive

Georgian Dublin Walk

Stroll back in time, passing some of the grandest Georgian buildings in Dublin. The squares provide a breath of fresh air in the city.

DISTANCE: 3km (2 miles) **ALLOW:** 2 hours plus stops

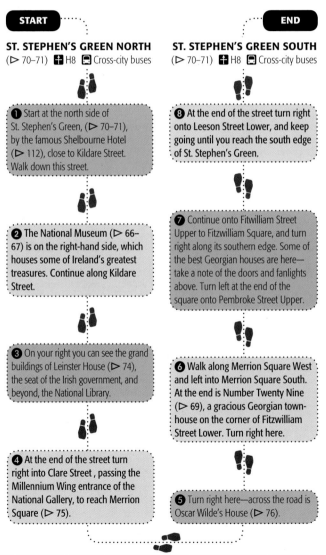

START

ST. STEPHEN'S GREEN NORTH
(▷ 70–71) ✚ H8 🚌 Cross-city buses

END

ST. STEPHEN'S GREEN SOUTH
(▷ 70–71) ✚ H8 🚌 Cross-city buses

① Start at the north side of St. Stephen's Green, (▷ 70–71), by the famous Shelbourne Hotel (▷ 112), close to Kildare Street. Walk down this street.

② The National Museum (▷ 66–67) is on the right-hand side, which houses some of Ireland's greatest treasures. Continue along Kildare Street.

③ On your right you can see the grand buildings of Leinster House (▷ 74), the seat of the Irish government, and beyond, the National Library.

④ At the end of the street turn right into Clare Street , passing the Millennium Wing entrance of the National Gallery, to reach Merrion Square (▷ 75).

⑧ At the end of the street turn right onto Leeson Street Lower, and keep going until you reach the south edge of St. Stephen's Green.

⑦ Continue onto Fitwilliam Street Upper to Fitzwilliam Square, and turn right along its southern edge. Some of the best Georgian houses are here—take a note of the doors and fanlights above. Turn left at the end of the square onto Pembroke Street Upper.

⑥ Walk along Merrion Square West and left into Merrion Square South. At the end is Number Twenty Nine (▷ 69), a gracious Georgian townhouse on the corner of Fitzwilliam Street Lower. Turn right here.

⑤ Turn right here—across the road is Oscar Wilde's House (▷ 76).

Shopping

ALIAS TOM
www.aliastom.com
One of Dublin's longest-standing men's stores, now with womenswear also. Armani, René Lezard and many, many more.
H7 ✉ Duke Lane
☎ 671 5443 🚉 Pearse
🚌 Cross-city buses

AVOCA
www.avoca.ie
One of Ireland's oldest surviving businesses, founded in 1723 and fast emerging as a fine department store for unique and exclusive high-quality items combining the traditional with the fashionable. The splendid food hall is packed with Irish delicacies including preserves, oils and biscuits, all under the Avoca label.
H7 ✉ 11–13 Suffolk Street ☎ 677 4215
🚉 Pearse 🚌 Cross-city buses

BROWN THOMAS
www.brownthomas.com
Ireland's stylish department store showcases Irish and international designer clothes. Also household furnishings, cosmetics, leather goods, accessories and linens.
H7 ✉ 88–95 Grafton Street ☎ 605 6666
🚉 Pearse 🚌 Cross-city buses

BT2
www.bt2.ie
Brown Thomas's trendy younger sibling sells more casual clothes like McQ,

Moschino and All Saints, with designer labels for men and women.
H7 ✉ 28–29 Grafton Street ☎ 605 6747
🚉 Pearse 🚌 Cross-city buses

BUTLER'S CHOCOLATE CAFÉ
www.butlerschocolates.com
Mouth-watering selection of Irish handmade chocolates from the original Mrs Bailey-Butler's recipe of 1932. Treat yourself!
H7 ✉ 51A Grafton Street ☎ 616 7004 🚉 Pearse
🚌 Cross-city buses

CATHACH BOOKS
www.rarebooks.ie
Dublin's leading rare and antiquarian bookshop, specializing in books of Irish interest, with a particular emphasis on 20th-century literature.

MADE IN IRELAND
If you're looking for something of modern Ireland for your home, check out the following:
Jerpoint glass—heavy, hand-blown pieces of simple design with color bursts. Waterford crystal—John Rocha's minimalist designer line has brought Waterford crystal bang up-to-date. Ceramics—look out for Nicholas Mosse's pottery and great designs by Louis Mulcahy, one of Ireland's most prolific ceramicists.

CELTIC NOTE
www.celticnote.com
One of the country's best specialist Irish music stores has everything from classical to traditional, rock to contemporary.
H7 ✉ 14 Nassau Street ☎ 670 4157 🚉 Pearse
🚌 Cross-city buses

CELTIC WHISKEY SHOP
www.celticwhiskeyshop.com
Tempting selection of Irish whiskeys, chocolates, liqueurs and wines. It has one of the best ranges of whiskeys in the city.
H7 ✉ 27–28 Dawson Street ☎ 675 9744
🚉 Pearse 🚌 Cross-city buses

CHARLES BYRNE
www.charlesbyrne.com
Established in 1870, Charles Byrne are renowned for their expertize in stringed instruments, and stock Ireland's best range of *bodhráns*, handmade by experts.
G7 ✉ 21–22 Stephen Street Lower ☎ 478 1773
🚉 Pearse 🚌 Cross-city buses

CLEO
www.cleo-ltd.com
If handknit sweaters, tweedy skirts and high-end country style is your style, Cleo's is the place for you. Run by the Joyce family since 1936, Cleo's specialize in natural fiber

clothes made in knitters' and weavers' homes.

THE DECENT CIGAR EMPORIUM

www.decent-cigar.com

All you would want to know and what to buy concerning the ultimate in cigars. Buy singly or by the box.

DESIGNYARD

www.designyard.ie

A venue for crafts and decorative arts. The stunning jewelry gallery showcases pieces by Irish designers made with both precious and non-precious materials. Lovely glass and ceramics too.

THE DRAWING ROOM

Ornate mahogany frames, embroidered cushions and richly decorated lampstands made from Chinese porcelain. Packed with gorgeous gifts and treats for the home.

DUBRAY BOOKS

www.dubraybooks.ie

Independent bookseller with three floors with an extensive collection of titles, including fiction, children, biographies and a section of Irish interest.

GALLERY 29

www.gallery29.ie

Irish-owned store selling vintage posters from the 1890s to 1990s, mainly advertising posters for food, travel and arts—all of them original. They can also mount and frame them for you.

HODGES FIGGIS

On four floors, this famous old bookstore was established in 1768 and is particularly revered

---

TRADITION LIVES ON

Irish traditional music is played in pubs all over the city every night of the week and is generally free. Music is often spontaneous, with musicians joining in an impromptu *seisún* (session). The Irish have grown up with this music; it has been handed down through the generations and instruments are often learned instinctively by watching others. All the traditional instruments and sheet music can be found in the excellent music shops across the city.

---

for its extensive collection of works on Celtic and Irish history, culture, art and literature.

HOUSE OF IRELAND

www.houseofireland.com

Traditional Irish fashion, crafts, Waterford crystal, Belleek china and Aran knitwear. Also the less well-known, attractive Galway crystal can be found here.

IB JORGENSEN FINE ART

www.jorgensenfineart.com

Ireland's most popular fashion designer turned to fine art in 1992 and hasn't looked back. Prepare to pay top prices for works by Mark Rode, Cody Swanson and Mary Swanzy. Also solo exhibitions of international contemporary artists.

JAMES FOX

www.jamesfox.ie

Established in 1881, this family-run specialist cigar and whiskey store stocks Ireland's largest selection of handmade Cuban cigars, complete with official Habanos certificates of authenticity. It's also a great place to find rare Irish single malt whiskeys.

✚ H7 ✉ 119 Grafton Street
☎ 677 0533 🚌 Cross-city buses; Luas St. Stephen's Green

JOHNSON'S COURT

An upmarket collection of top-notch jewelry shops nestled in a small alleyway. Choose from a range of goods, from luxury watches at Paul Sheeran to rings at Donovan & Matson.
✚ H7 ✉ Off Grafton Street
🚌 Cross-city buses; Luas St. Stephen's Green

KERLIN GALLERY

www.kerlin.ie
This is arguably Dublin's leading contemporary art gallery, established in 1988, showcasing the work of top artists like Dorothy Cross, Feilim Egan, David Godbold and Paul Seawright.
✚ H7 ✉ Anne's Lane, off Anne Street South
☎ 670 9093 🚊 Pearse
🚌 Cross-city buses

KEVIN AND HOWLIN

www.kelvinandhowlin.com
Shop here for your Donegal tweeds. All the usual hardwearing items—jackets, waistcoats, hats and ties in both modern and traditional styles. They last for years.
✚ H7 ✉ 31 Nassau Street
☎ 633 4576 🚊 Pearse
🚌 Cross-city buses

KILKENNY

www.kilkennyshop.com
This large emporium sells stylish Irish decorative objects. Waterford crystal, books, fashion and Celtic-inspired jewelry, with traditional yet creative pieces from designers such as Orla Kiely. Great café-restaurant overlooking Trinity college's grounds.
✚ H7 ✉ 6–15 Nassau Street ☎ 677 7066
🚊 Pearse 🚌 Cross-city buses

KNOBS AND KNOCKERS

www.knobsandknockers.ie
Everything you could think of to furnish your door. The Irish Claddagh knocker, based on the symbolic 'friendship, loyalty and love' Claddagh ring, is one of the most popular lines.
✚ H7 ✉ 19 Nassau Street
☎ 671 0288 🚊 Pearse
🚌 Cross-city buses

WHAT'S YOUR STYLE

There are some great shops in Dublin displaying a wide range of home interior products, many produced by Irish craftspeople and also by fashion designers turning to objects and furniture. Interior design is popular worldwide, and Dublin is gaining more shops for the enthusiast. Beautiful items in stone, wood, glass and other natural materials can be bought in both traditional and contemporary styles. Terence Conran, John Rocha and other well-known names.

LOUIS COPELAND

www.louiscopeland.com
A Louis Copeland suit, made-to-measure or off the peg, is a rite of passage for well-dressed Irish men. Chosen by politicians and society figures.
✚ J8 ✉ 30 Pembroke Street Lower ☎ 6610110 🚌 10

LOUISE KENNEDY

www.louisekennedy.com
Kennedy's tasteful, exclusive clothing and crystal collections are sold alongside luxury branded accessories and gorgeous gifts to take home.
✚ J8 ✉ 56 Merrion Square
☎ 662 0056 🚊 Pearse
🚌 Cross-city buses

MAGILLS

Salami, meats, bread, cheese, coffee, herbs, spices and every sort of delicacy are crammed into this atmospheric deli.
✚ H7 ✉ 14 Clarendon Street ☎ 671 3830
🚊 Pearse 🚌 Cross-city buses

MARKS & SPENCER

A branch of the famous UK-based chain selling all its usual men's, women's, and children's ranges and homeware, located in a lovely building.
✚ H7 ✉ 15–20 Grafton Street ☎ 679 7855
🚊 Pearse 🚌 Cross-city buses

PAMELA SCOTT

www.pamelascott.ie
One of Grafton Street's few Irish-owned fashion emporiums, this branch stocks dozens of leading

fashion labels such as Olsen, Tommy Hilfiger and Betty Barclay.
H7 ✉ 84 Grafton Street ☎ 679 6655 🚌 Cross-city buses; Luas St. Stephen's Green

ST. STEPHEN'S GREEN CENTRE
www.stephensgreen.com
A light, airy complex over three floors with good parking. The mall combines more expensive specialist shops with Dunnes department store and bargain emporia.
H8 ✉ Top of Grafton Street ☎ 478 0888 🚉 Pearse 🚌 Cross-city bus

SECRET BOOK & RECORD STORE
Tucked-away, this much-loved Dublin gem sells second-hand paperbacks, classic novels, modern art books and even records.
H7 ✉ 15a Wicklow Street ☎ 679 7272 🚌 Cross-city buses; Luas St. Stephen's Greens

SHERIDANS CHEESE SHOP
www.sheridanscheesemongers.com
This glorious shop packed with blocks of cheese is a wonderful showcase for Irish farmhouse varieties that are winning awards worldwide. The shop also sells Irish foods such as salmon and marmalades.
H8 ✉ 11 Anne Street South ☎ 679 3143 🚉 Pearse 🚌 Cross-city buses

SILVER SHOP
www.silvershopdublin.com
A wide range of antique silver and silver-plate from the conventional to the unusual Irish portrait miniatures. Prices start low and head up into the thousands.
H7 ✉ Second Floor, Powerscourt Centre, 59 South William Street ☎ 679 4147 🚉 Pearse 🚌 Cross-city buses

STOCK
Furniture, fabrics, rugs, lighting and an impressive range of kitchen utensils and cookware are on offer here. Serious cooks will come across more unusual items that can be hard to find elsewhere.
H8 ✉ 33–34 King Street South ☎ 679 4316 🚉 Pearse 🚌 Cross-city buses

IRELAND'S INTERNATIONAL DESIGNERS

Dublin fashion stores carry a great mix of contemporary, alternative and classic collections. Irish designers to look for include John Rocha, Paul Costelloe, Lainey Keogh, Daryl Kerrigan and Philip Treacy. Check out the handbags by Helen Cody and Orla Kiely, Vivienne Walsh's intricate jewelry, Pauric Sweeney's witty postmodern accessories stocked at Hobo and Slim Barrett's quirky fairy-tale tiaras.

SUSAN HUNTER
www.susanhunterlingerie.ie
Tiny but exclusive lingerie store. Luxury brands include La Perla and Tuttabankem.
H7 ✉ 13 Westbury Mall, off Grafton Street ☎ 679 1271 🚉 Pearse 🚌 Cross-city buses

TRIBE
www.tribe-clothing.com
A special shop for Ireland's urban skaters and surfers, Karl Swan's laid-back store is crammed with casual clothes and accessories.
H8 ✉ First floor, St. Stephen's Green Centre ☎ 475 0311 🚉 Pearse 🚌 Cross-city buses

TRINITY SWEATERS
www.thesweatershop.ie
The knitted Aran sweaters, Merino-wool ponchos, cashmere capes and Celtic scarves would make a great addition to anyone's wardrobe.
H7 ✉ 30 Nassau Street ☎ 671 2292 🚌 Cross-city buses; Luas St. Stephen's Green

WEIR & SONS
www.weirandsons.ie
Founded in 1869, this family-run business is one of Grafton Street's most-well-established shops. Top jewelry brands, including antique silver, are matched by exquisite service.
H7 ✉ 96–99 Grafton Street ☎ 677 9678 🚌 Cross-city buses; Luas St. Stephen's Green

Entertainment and Nightlife

BRUXELLES

www.bruxelles.ie

Three bars in one, tucked away off Grafton Street. Most nights see live rock bands, plus regular DJ nights. There's a big screen showing major sports events, and a convivial saloon bar with a proud music heritage.

➕ H7 ✉ 7 Harry Street
☎ 677 5362 🚌 Cross-city buses; Luas St. Stephen's Green

CAFÉ EN SEINE

www.cafeenseine.ie

The beautiful interior of this long bar has strikingly high ceilings supporting French bistro lighting. The relaxed daytime atmosphere hots up in the evening and lines form after 11pm on weekends.

➕ H7 ✉ 39 Dawson Street
☎ 677 4567 🚇 Pearse
🚌 Cross-city buses

CAPTAIN AMERICA'S COOKHOUSE AND BAR

www.captainamericas.com

This is a lively American-style bar and diner that was established here in 1971. Since then it has amassed a huge collection of Irish and international rock and roll memorabilia. The walls are hung with nostalgia items from the likes of U2, REM and the Rolling Stones. Be prepared for crowds—especially on Saturday.

➕ H7 ✉ 44 Grafton Street
☎ 671 5266 🚇 Pearse
🚌 Cross-city buses

DOHENY AND NESBITT

www.dohenyandnesbitt.com

A distinguished old pub that attracts politicians and media people to its three floors and bars well-stocked with whiskeys and stouts. Victorian-style mirrored walls, high ceilings and intimate snugs reflect its 19th-century origins.

➕ J8 ✉ 5 Baggot Street Lower ☎ 676 2945 🚌 10, 15X, 25X, 49X

GAIETY THEATRE

www.gaietytheatre.ie

An integral part of Dublin theaterland, staging opera, musicals, classic plays, comedies, pantomime and touring shows. After a major refurbishment, the Gaiety's agenda is ambitious. Hear lunchtime arias during the opera season.

TOP TALENT

Dublin, Ireland's literary and artistic capital, overflows with theatrical talent. Riverdance and *Dancing at Lughnasa* both played to Irish audiences before receiving global acclaim, and Martin McDonagh packed Dubliners in to see his Lenane trilogy prior to winning several Tony awards on Broadway. In contrast, the city's annual Christmas pantomimes see Irish celebrities ham up traditional tales.

➕ H8 ✉ King Street South
☎ 456 9569 🚇 Pearse
🚌 Cross-city buses

THE HORSESHOE BAR

www.marriott.co.uk

Over the decades, many a famous face has sat down in the bar of the grand Shelbourne Hotel (➤ 112) to enjoy a drink. Try a Black Velvet cocktail, made from Champagne and Guinness, said to have been created here.

➕ H8 ✉ The Shelbourne Dublin, 27 St. Stephen's Green ☎ 663 4500 🚌 Cross-city buses; Luas St. Stephen's Green

INTERNATIONAL BAR

www.international-bar.com

Indulge in a hefty helping of Irish wit at the home of the Comedy Cellar, founded by comic geniuses Ardal O'Hanlon, Dylan Moran and others. The daily evening schedule of events includes blues and country music as well as comedy.

➕ H7 ✉ 23 Wicklow Street
☎ 677 9250 🚇 Pearse
🚌 Cross-city buses

J.W. SWEETMAN

www.jwsweetman.ie

If you fancy a change from Guinness try the excellent beers at this microbrewery. Unique beers plus good food daily until 9.30pm.

➕ H6 ✉ 1–2 Burgh Quay
☎ 670 5777 🚇 Tara Street
🚌 Cross-city buses

LILLIE'S BORDELLO

www.lilliesbordello.ie

A home-away-from-home for pop and movie stars. House, garage, chart R&B, funk and mainstream pop and club classics.

🚻 H7 ✉ Adam Court, Grafton Street ☎ 679 9204 🚉 Pearse 🚌 Cross-city buses

MCDAID'S

McDaid's is a Dublin literary institution—all wood and stained glass. It was here that the likes of Brendan Behan, Patrick Kavanagh and Flann O'Brien relaxed in their local. It gets crowded but has a great atmosphere.

🚻 H7 ✉ 3 Harry Street ☎ 679 4395 🚉 Pearse 🚌 Cross-city buses

MULLIGANS

www.mulligans.ie

A pub since 1820, Mulligans is a Guinness drinker's institution. Retaining its Victorian mahogany furnishings, it has resisted change.

🚻 H6 ✉ 8 Poolbeg Street ☎ 677 5582 🚉 Tara Street 🚌 Cross-city buses

NATIONAL CONCERT HALL

www.nch.ie

Busy Georgian concert hall with a modern 250-seat auditorium and world-class acoustics that is home to the RTÉ National Symphony Orchestra. Top artists perform here. Plans are in motion for a major redevelopment of the concert hall.

🚻 H9 ✉ Earlsfort Terrace ☎ 417 0000 🚉 Pearse 🚌 14, 14A, 15A, 44, 74

O'DONOGHUE'S

www.odonoghues.ie

Renowned for its associations with the famous folk group the Dubliners, O'Donoghue's is a good place for impromptu sessions but it does get crowded.

🚻 J8 ✉ 15 Merrion Row ☎ 660 7194 🚉 Pearse 🚌 Cross-city buses

O'NEILLS

www.oneillsdublin.com

O'Neills always offers a friendly welcome. It is renowned for its ageless character and numerous alcoves and snugs. Good for the *craic* and some tasty food.

THE CLASSICS

Dublin has a thriving classical music and opera scene, though performances are irregular. The National Concert Hall stages a full schedule but other venues offer seasonal performances only. The Gaiety Theatre plays host to Dublin's most professional and prolific opera society. To find out about forthcoming events, call the box offices direct or check the listings in the *Irish Times*. Reservations are recommended for most of the performances.

🚻 J7 ✉ 36–37 Pearse Street ☎ 671 4074 🚉 Pearse 🚌 Cross-city buses

POD

www.pod.ie

The Place of Dance is one of the hippest clubs in town. Different club each evening but a good mix of happy house and popular dance floor hits. Try the hip Lobby Bar for a drink before hitting Crawdaddy or Tripod clubs, all on the same premises.

🚻 G9 ✉ Old Harcourt Station, 35 Harcourt Street ☎ 4776 3374 🚌 Cross-city buses; Luas Harcourt

THE SCHOOLHOUSE BAR

www.schoolhousehotel.com

Set in a lovely hotel in the fashionable Ballsbridge neighborhood. The building, a converted school, keeps many of its original features. Food is served all day, and there is live music Thursday to Saturday. Small garden.

🚻 K8 ✉ 2–8 Northumberland Road ☎ 667 5014 🚉 DART Grand Canal Dock

THE SUGAR CLUB

www.thesugarclub.com

In a converted cinema, this multi-purpose arts center has regular live bands, DJ nights and occasional film screenings.

🚻 H9 ✉ 8 Leeson Street Lower ☎ 678 7188 🚉 Pearse 🚌 10, 11, 14, 15, 44, 46, 86

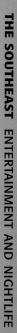

THE SOUTHEAST ENTERTAINMENT AND NIGHTLIFE

Restaurants

PRICES

Prices are approximate, based on a 3-course meal for one person.

€€€	over €40
€€	€25–€40
€	under €25

BANG RESTAURANT (€€)

www.bangrestaurant.com
Cool and minimal, Bang is as trendy and fresh as its get-ahead clientele, and its eclectic, modern European menu is as fashionable as its chic, cosmopolitan interiors.
➕ J8 ✉ 11 Merrion Row ☎ 400 4229 🕐 Lunch, dinner Mon–Sat 🚃 Pearse 🚌 Cross-city buses

THE BANK ON COLLEGE GREEN (€)

www.bankoncollegegreen.com
The former banking hall of the Belfast Bank is a spectacular setting for good-value, all-day food. Take a balcony table for a view of the mosaics, plasterwork, carved wood and stained-glass ceiling.
➕ H7 ✉ 20–22 College Green ☎ 677 0677 🕐 Breakfast, lunch and dinner daily 🚃 Pearse 🚌 Cross-city buses

BEWLEY'S CAFÉ (€)

www.bewleys.com
Steeped in history, tradition and nostalgia, Bewley's has glorious wood-paneled rooms, stained-glass windows and artworks on the walls. Fairtrade coffee is freshly ground on the premises. In the Café Theatre lunch-time drama and literary readings are regular events, and there is also evening cabaret.
➕ H7 ✉ 78 Grafton Street ☎ 672 7720 🕐 Mon–Wed 8am–10pm, Thu–Sat 8am–11pm, Sun 9am–10pm 🚃 Pearse 🚌 Cross-city buses

CHILI CLUB (€€)

www.chiliclub.ie
This tiny, simple restaurant is loved for its fiery Thai curries, plus fresh stir-fried shrimp in ginger, pad Thai and tangy Thai soups. The fixed-price set menu is very reasonable.
➕ H7 ✉ 1 Anne's Lane, off Anne Street South ☎ 677 3721 🕐 Lunch Wed–Fri, dinner Tue–Sun 🚃 Pearse 🚌 Cross-city buses

TIPS FOR EATING OUT

● Eating out is extremely popular in Dublin, so reserve ahead. Some restaurants close on Monday. Most serious restaurants offer a fixed-price lunch menu that represents excellent value.

● Early-bird meals are popular, a value meal usually served before 7pm.

● A service charge of 12.5 per cent may be added to your bill, especially if a group of people are dining. If service is not included, a sum of 12.5–15 per cent is the usual added tip.

CORNUCOPIA (€)

www.cornucopia.ie
Wholefood and vegetarian dishes served in a sunny dining room. Home-made dishes from breakfast through to dinner, with fresh salads, hot stews and delicious cakes; plus vegan dishes.
➕ H7 ✉ 19 Wicklow Street ☎ 677 7583 🕐 Breakfast, lunch and dinner Mon–Sat (Sun 12–9) 🚃 Pearse 🚌 Cross-city buses

DAX (€€€)

www.dax.ie
For over a decade this renowned Irish-French restaurant has been serving food in an intimate basement in a Georgian building. Its ever-changing seven-course menu may include the likes of Wicklow venison loin in red wine jus and sea bream with braised seaweed.
➕ J9 ✉ 23 Pembroke Street Upper ☎ 676 1494 🕐 Lunch Tue–Fri, dinner Tue–Sat 🚃 11, 11A, 46; Luas Harcourt

DIEP LE SHAKER (€€–€€€)

www.diep.net
A stylish haunt offering some of the best, most beautifully presented and tastiest Thai cuisine in Ireland. The surroundings are sophisticated, with a vibrant atmosphere.
➕ J8 ✉ 55 Pembroke Lane ☎ 661 1829 🕐 Lunch Tue–Fri, dinner Tue–Sat 🚃 Lansdowne Road 🚌 Cross-city buses

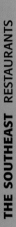

DUNNE & CRESCENZI (€€)

www.dunneandcrescenzi.com
Authentic Italian bistro, part of the Slow Food Revolution. Enjoy the relaxed atmosphere, well prepared food made with quality ingredients, and good Italian wines.
🚩 H7 ✉ 14–16 Frederick Street South ☎ 675 9892 🕓 All day dining 🚉 Pearse 🚌 Cross-city buses

L'ECRIVAIN (€€€)

www.lecrivain.com
Chef Derry Clarke's popular Michelin-starred Irish modern restaurant continues to grow in stature. It is well known for its fresh fish, which is caught all over Ireland on the same day. Friendly service.
🚩 J8 ✉ 109a Lower Baggot Street ☎ 661 1919 🕓 Lunch Thu–Fri, dinner Mon–Sat 🚌 10

THE FARM (€€)

www.thefarmfood.ie
With outside seating, great for people-watching on Dawson Street, this restaurant serves healthy, organic Irish products. Farm charcuterie, home-smoked duck breast and wild Irish game pie are some of the dishes on its regularly changing menu. Good vegetarian selection.
🚩 H7 ✉ 3 Dawson Street ☎ 671 8654 🕓 Lunch and dinner daily 🚌 Cross-city buses; Luas St. Stephen's Green

FIRE (€€€)

www.mansionhouse.ie
The spacious dining room is set in the resplendent belle époque era. A modern European menu with a twist. Jumbo tiger prawns from the wood-fired oven and prime steaks are the signature dishes. Pre-theater meals are good value.
🚩 H8 ✉ The Mansion House, Dawson Street ☎ 676 7200 🕓 Dinner daily 🚌 Cross-city buses

THE GALLERY (€€)

www.doylecollection.com
Located in the Westbury Hotel (➤ 112), this is the perfect place for afternoon tea with great views of Grafton Street and a €1 million Irish art collection. Just kick back, relax and enjoy.

PUB GRUB

Pubs in Dublin are synonymous with drinking, Guinness, traditional Irish music and good *craic*. But pub food is popular and, particularly for those on a limited budget, good value. You can get some excellent hearty meals, including traditional Irish stews, the boxty (potato pancake) and colcannon (cabbage and potato). There is often a carvery offering a choice of salads. Sample any of these accompanied by a pint of Guinness to be like a local.

🚩 H7 ✉ Grafton Street ☎ 679 1122 🕓 Afternoon tea 3pm–5.30pm 🚉 Pearse 🚌 Cross-city buses

THE GOTHAM CAFÉ (€–€€)

www.gothamcafe.ie
Lively, family-friendly café-restaurant famed for its pizzas. Imaginative toppings; plus pasta and vegetarian dishes, huge salads and a kids' menu. Its walls are adorned with covers of *Rolling Stone* magazine.
🚩 H7 ✉ 8 Anne Street South ☎ 679 5266 🕓 Lunch and dinner daily 🚌 Cross-city buses; Luas St. Stephen's Green

HATCH & SONS IRISH KITCHEN (€–€€)

www.hatchandsons.co
A welcoming café-restaurant inside the Little Museum of Dublin (➤ 74), which celebrates fresh Irish ingredients. Traditional dishes on the menu include beef and Guinness stew, smoked fish platters and fresh sandwiches. A few craft beers make a good accompaniment.
🚩 H8 ✉ 15 St. Stephen's Green ☎ 661 0075 🕓 Breakfast, lunch and early evening daily 🚌 Cross-city buses; Luas St. Stephen's Green

KEOGHS (€)

Great for snacks, paninis and food to take out. Try the tasty home-baked scones. There's also a

nice range of coffees and tangy, freshly squeezed, orange juice.

➕ H7 ✉ 1–2 Trinity Street ☎ 677 8599 🕐 Daily 🚉 Pearse 🚌 Cross-city buses

LANGKAWI (€€)

www.langkawi.ie
Excellent Malaysian restaurant with an exciting, extensive menu. Totally delicious food that's high on taste.

➕ K9 ✉ 46 Baggot Street Upper ☎ 668 2760 🕐 Lunch Mon–Fri, dinner daily 🚉 Lansdowne Road 🚌 10

MAO (€–€€)

www.mymao.ie
Enjoy fresh, authentic Thai, Malaysian and Indonesian dishes in contemporary surroundings.

➕ H7 ✉ 2 Chatham Row ☎ 670 4899 🕐 Lunch and dinner daily 🚉 Pearse 🚌 Cross-city buses

MARCO PIERRE WHITE STEAKHOUSE & GRILL (€€€)

www.marcopierrewhite.ie
Simple food beautifully cooked and presented. Top quality in every way. Lunch and pre-theater menus are great value.

➕ H8 ✉ 51 Dawson Street ☎ 677 1155 🕐 Lunch and dinner daily 🚉 Pearse 🚌 Cross-city buses

LA MÈRE ZOU (€€–€€€)

www.lamerezou.ie
Welcoming basement restaurant serving good classic Franco-Belgian cuisine. A long-time city favorite. Live jazz on Friday and Saturday.

➕ H8 ✉ 22 St. Stephen's Green ☎ 661 6669 🕐 Lunch Mon–Fri, dinner daily 🚉 Pearse 🚌 Cross-city buses

PASTA FRESCA (€)

www.pastafresca.ie
A friendly, busy restaurant dishing up excellent home-made fresh pasta and pizzas until late.

➕ H7 ✉ 2–4 Chatham Street ☎ 679 2402 🕐 Lunch and dinner daily 🚉 Pearse 🚌 Cross-city buses

PEARL BRASSERIE (€€€)

www.pearl-brasserie.com
Classy restaurant with romantic alcoves, oyster bar, modern art and an inventive menu that

includes fine fish and game dishes. Friendly and attentive staff.

➕ J8 ✉ 20 Merrion Street Upper ☎ 661 3572 🕐 Lunch Mon–Fri, dinner Mon–Sat 🚉 Pearse 🚌 Cross-city buses

LA PENICHE (€€)

www.lapeniche.ie
La Peniche is on a barge which cruises the Dublin Canal, or may stay moored up. Either way it's a good alternative eating venue. The food is French/Italian bistro style; simple but local and organic produce is used with excellent results. Fully licensed, serving French wines, beers and ciders.

➕ J9 ✉ Grand Canal, Mespil Road ☎ 087 790 0077 (mobile) 🕐 Dinner Wed–Sun 🚉 Grand Canal Dock 🚌 10, 10A, 18

THE PIG'S EAR (€–€€)

www.thepigsear.ie
This upstairs restaurant overlooks Trinity College. The celebrity TV chef, Stephen McAllister, cooks contemporary Irish food. It's an informal, friendly restaurant offering thrifty lunch and early evening set menus. There's also a third-floor Chef's Counter 16-course tasting menu for groups of 6 or more.

➕ H7 ✉ 4 Nassau Street ☎ 670 3865 🕐 Lunch and dinner Mon–Sat, also breakfast May–Sep 🚉 Pearse 🚌 Cross-city buses

RESTAURANT PATRICK GUILBAUD (€€€)

www.restaurantpatrick guilbaud.ie

Superlative fine dining by French chef Guillaume Lebrun. Desserts to die for. A tastefully decorated restaurant and a wonderful collection of Irish art.

✚ J8 ✉ 21 Merrion Street Upper ☎ 676 4192 ⊙ Lunch and dinner Tue–Sat 🚆 Pearse 🚌 Cross-city buses

SABA (€€)

www.sabadublin.com

Serving first-class Thai and Vietnamese food using organic and Fairtrade ingredients, the setting at Saba (meaning 'happy meeting place') is stylish. The executive chef has cooked for the Thai royal family.

✚ H7 ✉ 26–28 Clarendon Street ☎ 679 2000 ⊙ Lunch and dinner daily 🚆 Pearse 🚌 Cross-city buses

SADDLE ROOM AND OYSTER BAR (€€€)

www.marriott.co.uk

The refurbished Shelbourne Hotel (▷ 112) has produced a smart contemporary dining experience. The Oyster Bar with its leather banquettes and intimate setting is one side of the opulent fine dining room. Seafood and steaks are the dish of the day, every day, cooked to perfection.

✚ H8 ✉ 27 St. Stephen's Green ☎ 663 4500

⊙ Breakfast, lunch and dinner daily 🚆 Pearse 🚌 Cross-city buses

SCIENCE GALLERY CAFÉ (€)

www.dublin.sciencegallery.com

Bright and breezy café inside the glass-and-steel Science Gallery at Trinity College. Breakfast, hot sandwiches and stone-baked pizza, plus a bar. Free WiFi.

✚ J7 ✉ Trinity College, Pearse Street ☎ 896 4091 ⊙ Breakfast, lunch and early evening daily 🚆 DART: Pearse Street 🚌 Cross-city buses

SHANAHAN'S ON THE GREEN (€€€)

www.shanahans.ie

A popular, highly regarded American steak and seafood restaurant, Shanahan's is set in an elegant Georgian house. Enjoy top cuts of Angus steak, and choose from one of the 5,000 wines from the extensive cellar. Excellent service.

✚ H8 ✉ 119 St. Stephen's Green ☎ 407 0939 ⊙ Lunch Friday; dinner Mon–Sat 🚌 Cross-city buses; Luas St. Stephen's Green

STEPS OF ROME (€)

Divine pizza by the slice, plus other gutsy Italian fare.

✚ H7 ✉ Chatham Court ☎ 670 5639 ⊙ Breakfast, lunch and dinner daily (Sun from 12) 🚆 Pearse 🚌 Cross-city buses

THORNTONS (€€€)

www.thorntonsrestaurant.com

Kevin Thornton has run his Michelin-starred restaurant here for over a decade, the epitome of high-end fine dining. The eight-course tasting menu is popular; the canapé lounge is less formal for a pre- or post-theater light bite with a glass of wine. A real treat.

✚ H8 ✉ Fitzwilliam Hotel, 128 St. Stephen's Green ☎ 478 7008 ⊙ Lunch Thu–Sat; dinner Tue–Sat 🚌 Cross-city buses; Luas St. Stephen's Green

WAGAMAMA (€€)

www.wagamama.ie

Fast and furious, churning out healthy substantial Japanese dishes in minimalist surroundings.

✚ H8 ✉ St. Stephen's Green Shopping Centre, King Street South ☎ 478 2152 ⊙ Lunch and dinner daily 🚆 Pearse 🚌 Cross-city buses

---

RAISING A GLASS

The Irish have a reputation for enjoying a tipple and it's not surprising given the quality of their native drinks. For stout sample Guinness or Murphy's. For whiskey— a traditional chaser to your stout—there's Jamesons or Bushmills. And don't forget the Baileys, made from two of Ireland's finest products— whiskey and cream.

Just a short distance outside Dublin the beautiful Irish countryside is a delight, with pretty seaside villages, stunning lakes and ancient Celtic burial sites. A trip to the suburbs can also be rewarding.

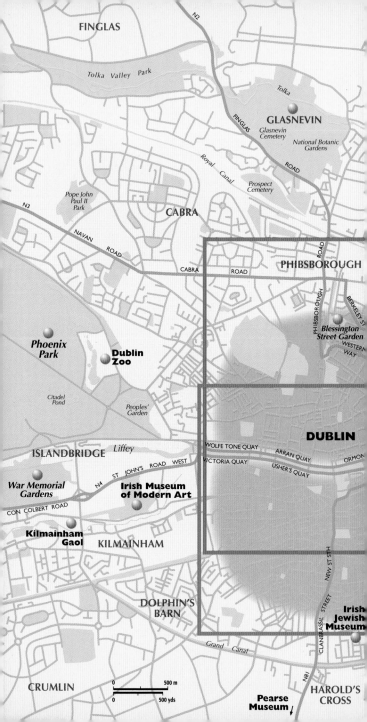

FINGLAS

N2

Tolka Valley Park

Tolka

GLASNEVIN

FINGLAS

Glasnevin Cemetery

National Botanic Gardens

ROAD

Royal Canal

Prospect Cemetery

N3

Pope John Paul II Park

CABRA

NAVAN ROAD

CABRA ROAD

PHIBSBOROUGH

PHIBSBOROUGH ROAD

BERKELEY ST

Blessington Street Garden

WESTERN WAY

Phoenix Park

Dublin Zoo

DUBLIN

Citadel Pond

Peoples' Garden

WOLFE TONE QUAY

ARRAN QUAY

ORMON

ISLANDBRIDGE

Liffey

VICTORIA QUAY

USHER'S QUAY

ST JOHN'S ROAD WEST

War Memorial Gardens

N4

Irish Museum of Modern Art

CON COLBERT ROAD

Kilmainham Gaol

KILMAINHAM

NEW ST STH

Irish Jewish Museum

DOLPHIN'S BARN

CLANBRASSIL STREET

Grand Canal

CRUMLIN

0   500 m
0   500 yds

Pearse Museum

N81

HAROLD'S CROSS

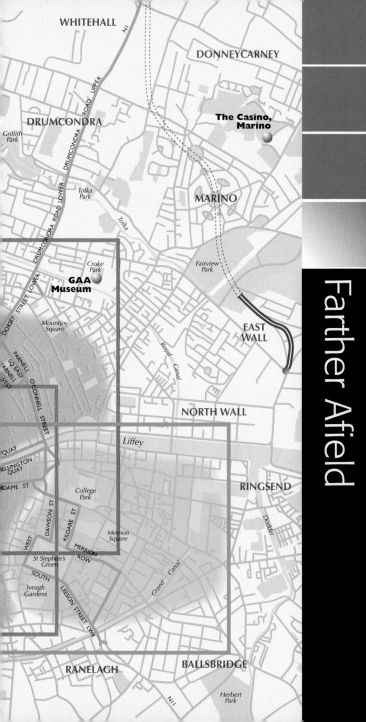

WHITEHALL

DONNEYCARNEY

N1

DRUMCONDRA

DRUMCONDRA ROAD UPPER

The Casino,
Marino

Griffith
Park

DRUMCONDRA ROAD LOWER

Tolka
Park

MARINO

Tolka

Croke
Park

Fairview
Park

**GAA
Museum**

DORSET STREET LOWER

Mountjoy
Square

EAST
WALL

Royal Canal

PARNELL
SQ EAST

PARNELL
WEST

O'CONNELL STREET

NORTH WALL

QUAY

Liffey

WELLINGTON
QUAY

DAME ST

College
Park

RINGSEND

Doddler

WEST

DAWSON ST

KILDARE ST

Merrion
Square

MERRION
ROW

St Stephen's
Green

SOUTH

Iveagh
Gardens

LEESON STREET LWR

Grand Canal

RANELAGH

BALLSBRIDGE

N11

Herbert
Park

Casino, Marino

The south-facing facade of the striking Casino at Marino, with its impressive columns

THE BASICS

www.heritageireland.ie

➕ M1

✉ Cherrymount Crescent, off the Malahide Road, Marino

☎ 833 1618

🕐 Mar–end Oct daily 10–5; last admission 45 min before closing

🚆 Clontarf Road

🚌 14, 20A, 20B, 27A

♿ Few

💷 Inexpensive

❓ Visit by guided tour only

HIGHLIGHTS

● Geometrical design
● Corner lions
● Curving wooden doors
● Stucco work
● Marquetry floors

The Mediterranean-inspired Casino, the work of Sir William Chambers, has to be the country's most compact and ingenious 18th-century architectural creation.

Inspiration The Casino is now surrounded by modern suburbia. But when viewed in its original rural setting, this deceptively small building must have resembled a Roman temple in Elysian fields. Its enlightened patron was James Caulfield, fourth Viscount Charlemont (1728–99), whose travels in the Mediterranean inspired him to re-create classical elegance and ingenuity in his homeland. To achieve this, he enticed King George III's architect, Sir William Chambers (1723–96), to design three buildings on his lands. Two survive: The first is his town house, now home to the Dublin City Gallery The Hugh Lane (▷ 49), and the second is this delightful house whose name derives from the Italian word *casa*. Curiously, Chambers never came to Ireland to see his masterpiece.

Geometry Its floor plan is a Greek cross encircled by pillars on a raised podium, with benign lions at each corner creating a diagonal axis. Columns are water pipes, urns are chimneys. What seems from the outside like a single interior space comprises 16 rooms. The four state rooms on the ground floor are perfect in detail—with curving wooden doors, stucco friezes illustrating musical instruments and agricultural implements, and fine marquetry floors carefully assembled with a variety of rare woods.

The O'Connell monument at Glasnevin (left); a Celtic cross in the cemetery (right)

Once the site of a monastery, this leafy suburb has two well-wooded neighbors separated only by a tall stone wall—the National Botanic Gardens and the National Cemetery.

Botanic Gardens Ireland's most extensive and varied collection of plants are carefully tended here. Laid out over 19.5ha (47 acres), the gardens were founded in 1795. The curvilinear glass houses, built by Richard Turner, a Dubliner who created a similar structure for Kew Gardens in London, are among the finest surviving examples of 19th-century glass-and-iron construction. Many of the plants housed within originate from southeast Asia. See herbaceous borders, alpines, roses, the rock garden, pond and arboretum. It is also home to 300 endangered plant species from around the world. There's a good education and visitor facility.

Cemetery The adjoining cemetery is reached by a separate entrance just over a mile away. Its graves are a Who's Who of modern Ireland's formative years: Charles Stewart Parnell, Michael Collins and Eamon de Valera to name but a few. Poet Gerard Manley Hopkins and writer Brendan Behan are also buried here. At the foot of Ireland's tallest Round Tower lie the remains of politican and engineer of Catholic Emancipation in Ireland, Daniel O'Connell (1775–1847), who founded the cemetery. The daily guided tours are fascinating, and the contemporary museum makes a visit even more worthwhile.

HIGHLIGHTS

Botanic Gardens
● Palm house
● Curvilinear glass house
● Last Rose of Summer

Cemetery
● O'Connell's tomb in crypt
● Parnell's grave
● Michael Collins' plot

Kilmainham Gaol

TOP
25

HIGHLIGHTS

● East wing
● 1916 corridor with cells
● Museum display

TIPS

● Ask the guide to shut you into one of the cells and find out what prison life was like.
● If you have limited time, miss out the audio-visual presentation as it is the least exciting part of the tour.

Leading figures in every rebellion against British rule since 1798 are associated with Kilmainham Gaol and, for many Irish people, their imprisonment or death represents freedom through sacrifice.

Prisoners A deserted gaol may seem an unusual place to spend a couple of hours, but with its stark and severe interiors, Kilmainham has a fascination that is more inspirational than morbid. Opened in 1796, and altered frequently since, the gaol is made up of tall interlinked blocks in the middle, flanked by exercise and work yards. During the course of its long history it held both civil and political prisoners, the earliest of whom were participants in the 1798 rebellion. The flow continued throughout the following century and included the 'Young Ireland' rebels of 1848 (Europe's 'Year of

Clockwise from top left: Detail of a cell door in Kilmainham Gaol, opened in 1796; a view of the main compound inside the gaol, which formerly housed generations of Irish rebels and is now a museum; the tree-lined pedestrian avenue leading to Kilmainham

Revolution'), the Fenian suspects of 1867 and notable parliamentarians in the 1880s.

Conditions Overcrowding created appalling conditions when the Great Famine of 1845–49 drove many to petty crime. Closed in 1910, the gaol was reopened during the 1916 rebellion in Dublin to receive insurgents whose execution in the prison in the May and June of that year turned the tide of public opinion in many parts of Ireland in favor of the armed struggle. During the Civil War of the early 1920s, the gaol again housed anti-government rebels including many women, and four Republican leaders were executed. The doors were closed in 1924, and the abandoned gaol was eventually restored between 1960 and 1984. Cared for by the State, it has an excellent museum display.

THE BASICS

www.heritageireland.ie

🔠 B7

✉ Inchicore Road, Kilmainham

☎ 453 5984

🕐 Apr–end Sep daily 9.30–6; Oct–end Mar Mon–Sat 9.30–5.30, Sun 10–6; last admission 1 hour before closing

🍴 Tea room

🚆 Heuston

🚌 51B, 78A, 79, 79A; Luas Suir Road

♿ Call in advance for wheelchair assistance

💷 Moderate

❓ Guided tours only. Prebook to avoid lines

Irish Museum of Modern Art

Gallery fountain (left); interior gallery (middle); Snowman by Gary Hume (right)

THE BASICS

www.imma.ie

🔁 C7

✉ Royal Hospital, Military Road, Kilmainham

☎ 612 9900

🕐 Tue–Sat 10–5.30 (except Wed 10.30–5.30), Sun and public hols 12–5.30

🍴 Café

🚆 Heuston

🚌 26, 51, 51B, 78A, 79, 90, 123; Luas Heuston

♿ Good

💷 Free

❓ Free guided tours every afternoon. Well-stocked bookshop

HIGHLIGHTS

● Covered arcade
● Courtyard with sculptures
● Permanent collections
● Visiting exhibitions

The Royal Hospital at Kilmainham, once a haven for retired soldiers, is now an ultramodern cultural hub where regularly changing exhibitions showcase the latest trends in contemporary art.

Shelter The most important surviving 17th-century building in Ireland, the Royal Hospital at Kilmainham was founded as the Irish equivalent of the Invalides in Paris and the Chelsea pensioners' hospital in London. The architect, surveyor-general Sir William Robinson, laid the structure around an open quadrangle, and created a covered arcade around three sides of the ground floor where residents could stroll out-doors even in poor weather.

Transformation A hospital until 1927, the building was restored in 1984 and eventually opened as the Irish Museum of Modern Art in 1991. IMMA is Ireland's leading national institution for the collection and preservation of modern and contemporary works of art. The Permanent Collection of 1,650 works reflects trends in Irish and international art, including installations, video art, sculpture and paintings. The Madden Arnholz Collection comprises old master prints by innovative European printmakers such as Dürer, Rembrandt, Goya and Hogarth, together with books containing prints by Thomas Bewick and his family and one of Bewick's printing blocks. The museum stages changing exhibitions of modern art from Europe and beyond, and is renowned for its education and community programmes.

BLESSINGTON STREET GARDEN

A 10-minute walk from O'Connell Street is the former city reservoir, Blessington Street Basin. Here you will find a quiet haven of peace for visitors and local wildlife. Landscaped in the mid-1990s, it remains largely undiscovered and is known as Dublin's secret garden.

➕ F4 ✉ Blessington Street ⏰ Daily during daylight hours 🚌 10 ✋ Free

DUBLIN ZOO

www.dublinzoo.ie

More than 700 animals from around the globe live in the zoo's 24ha (60 acres), many with plenty of room to roam. Visit Monkey Island, the Arctic Fringes and the World of the Primates, and don't miss the Pet Care Area, Reptile House and Discovery Centre. Spot giraffes and zebras on the Plains of Africa and Asian elephants in the Rainforest. Check out the keeper talks and feeding times.

➕ B5 ✉ Phoenix Park ☎ 474 8900 ⏰ Mar–Sep daily 9.30–6; Oct 9.30–5.30; Nov, Dec 9.30–4; Jan 9.30–4.30 🚌 10, 10A, 25, 26, 66, 66A, 66B, 67, 67A; Luas Heuston 🍴 Restaurant, cafés ♿ Good ✋ Expensive

GAA MUSEUM

www.crokepark.ie/gaa-museum

The Gaelic Athletic Association (GAA) is Ireland's largest sporting and cultural organization. Their museum, dedicated to the national games, is housed in the home of Gaelic sport, Croke Park, and is well worth a visit. It focuses on the history of Gaelic games and players, has changing exhibitions, numerous medal collections and over 40 audio-visual shows. Guided museum and stadium tours are available year round.

➕ J3 ✉ Cusack Stand, Croke Park, St. Joseph's Avenue ☎ 819 2323 ⏰ Jun–Aug Mon–Sat 9.30–6, Sun 10.30–5; Sep–May 9.30–5, Sun 10.30–5; not open to general public on match days 🚌 1, 11, 13, 33, 41 ✋ Expensive

IRISH JEWISH MUSEUM

The museum is dedicated to the history of the Jewish community in Ireland from the mid-19th century to

Resting on one leg–a stork in the zoo

Meet the elephants at Dublin Zoo

the present day. The original kitchen re-creates a typical Sabbath meal of the early 20th century. An expansion announced in late 2013 may entail closures.

🏠 G9 ✉ 4 Walworth Road, off Victoria Street ☎ 490 1857 🕐 Nov–end Apr Sun only 11–3; May–end Oct Sun–Thu 11–3.30 🚍 16, 16A, 19, 19A, 122 ♿ Few 🎫 Free

PEARSE MUSEUM

www.heritageireland.ie

This former school was run by Patrick Pearse, the Dublin-born poet and revolutionary executed in 1916 at Kilmainham Gaol (▷ 94–95). Set in beautiful grounds, it has a nature study room displaying Irish fauna and flora. Concerts are held here in summer. The museum is in St. Enda's Park, which has riverside walks, a waterfall and walled garden.

🏠 Off map at F9 ✉ St. Enda's Park, Grange Road, Rathfarnham ☎ 493 4208 🕐 Mar–Oct Mon–Sat 9.30–5; Nov–Jan 9.30–4; Feb 9.30–5, Sun and public hols from 10. Closed Tue year round 🚍 16 🍴 Tea rooms ♿ Ground floor 🎫 Free

PHOENIX PARK AND NATURE STUDY CENTRE

www.phoenixpark.ie

A vast expanse of green space, lakes and woodland in the heart of the city, this is one of the largest urban parks in Europe, covering some 707ha (1,747 acres) and encircled by a 13km (8-mile) wall. Within its confines are Dublin Zoo (▷ 97), the American Ambassador's home and the Irish President's residence. Bicycles are available to rent.

🏠 A5 ☎ 677 0095 🚍 37, 38, 39; Luas Heuston (Parkgate Street entrance) 🎫 Free

WAR MEMORIAL GARDENS

www.heritageireland.ie

These gardens are dedicated to the 49,400 Irish soldiers who died in World War I. Especially moving are the thousands of names etched in the granite book rooms, and the beautiful sunken rose gardens.

🏠 A7 ✉ Islandbridge ☎ 475 7816 🕐 Mon–Fri 8–dusk, Sat–Sun 10–dusk 🚍 51, 68, 69 🎫 Free

Golden harp at the Memorial Gardens (above); mural at the Setanta Centre (right)

Dublin from the DART

VIEWS FROM THE DART

- Dalkey Island off Killiney
- Sailboats off Dun Laoghaire
- Blackrock's public park and private gardens
- Wetlands bird sanctuary at Booterstown
- Custom House between Tara Street and Connolly Station
- Urban jungle of Kilbarrack, backdrop for novels *The Commitments*, *The Snapper* and *The Van*, Roddy Doyle's prize-winning trilogy

BRAY

This attractive seaside town, toward the southern end of the DART line, has long been a popular holiday resort enjoyed for its sandy beach and mile-long promenade. The Jazz Festival in May and Summerfest in July and August bring in the crowds. There are fine walks and splendid views around nearby Bray Head.

DUN LAOGHAIRE

Invigorating walks along the piers at Dun Laoghaire, a Victorian seaside resort once known as Kingstown, are something of a Dublin institution. The scenery is stunning, and you can see the ferries plying across the Irish Sea. The East Pier, popular with walkers, featured in the 1996 film *Michael Collins* and has a lighthouse at the end. The longer West Pier attracts fishing enthusiasts.

HOWTH

This promontory to the north of Dublin is a traditional fishing village and trendy suburb in one. A popular sailing hub, the marina is always packed with yachts from Ireland and abroad. Howth DART station is near the harbor and close to all the waterside activity, bars and restaurants. Howth is idyllic in sunny weather, and gets very busy at weekends with Dubliners walking to Howth Head.

Fishing boats in the harbor at Howth

Bray Head promenade (above right); Kilruddery House, Bray (right)

KILLINEY

National and international celebrities such as Bono, Damon Hill, Neil Jordan, Enya, and Eddie Irvine have lived in the resort known affectionately as Dublin's Riviera. Take a walk along the Vico Road for what is arguably the most breathtaking view in Dublin. Look out to Dalkey Island, a craggy piece of land captured by the Vikings and later the site of Christian communities. Fishermen in nearby Coliemore Harbour run boat trips in summer to view the resident goats, the ruined oratory and the Martello tower.

SANDYCOVE

Just south of Dun Laoghaire and accessible by the DART is the popular commuter village of Sandycove, famous for its seaside promenade, which runs all the way to Dun Laoghaire. It is named after a small sandy cove near the rocky point on which a Martello tower was built during the Napoleonic Wars. James Joyce chose the Martello tower along the waterfront as the setting for the first chapter of *Ulysses*, and the museum inside displays Joycean memorabilia (tel 280 9265; www.jamesjoycetower.com for opening times). A bracing swim in the sea here may introduce you to other die-hards who take the plunge all year around.

DALKEY

Travel only a few stops south on the DART and you'll find yourself in the attractive former fishing village of Dalkey, well known for its literary associations. George Bernard Shaw lived in the village and James Joyce set chapter two of *Ulyssess* here. The Heritage Centre is accessed through Goat Castle in Castle Street and from the battlements you get a splendid view of the sea and mountains. Good pubs and restaurants enhance your visit.

View from Dalkey Hill across Killiney Bay toward the distant Wicklow hills

St. Kevin's Church, Glendalough (▷ 102)

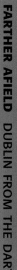

Excursions

THE BASICS

www.heritageireland.ie
Distance: 64km (40 miles)
Journey Time: 1 hour
30 min
✉ Brú Na Bóinne Visitor
Centre, Donore, Co Meath
☎ 041 988 0300
🕐 Daily; check for
opening times
🚌 Bus Éireann 100 to
Drogheda, then 163 to
Donore village (10-min
walk). Also bus tours

BRÚ NA BÓINNE

**A designated UNESCO World Heritage
Site, Brú Na Bóinne is one of the most
important prehistoric monuments in
Europe.**

'The Palace of the Boyne' is the name given
to a large group of neolithic remains in the
central Boyne Valley 11km (7 miles) west of
Drogheda. The huge, white-fronted passage
tomb of Newgrange is the best known, but the
nearby mounds of Knowth and Dowth were
probably of equal importance historically. These
great tombs are more than 5,000 years old.
You can only visit the main site with a tour from
the visitor center.

THE BASICS

www.glendalough.ie
Distance: 48km (30 miles)
Journey Time: 1 hour
15 min
☎ 404 45325
🕐 Visitor center mid-Mar
to mid-Oct daily 9.30–6;
mid-Oct to mid-Mar 9.30–5;
last admission 45 min
before closing
🚌 St. Kevin's bus from
Bray and Dublin. Can be
reached on coach tours
from Dublin. The most
direct route if driving is the
N11 (M11) south

GLENDALOUGH

**Glendalough ('valley of two lakes') was
one of Ireland's most venerated monasteries. Its setting makes it one of eastern
Ireland's premier attractions.**

Situated at the end of a long valley stretching
deep into the Wicklow Mountains, Glendalough
grew up around the tomb of its founder, St. Kevin.
He was abbot until his death in AD618 and the
monastery became famous throughout Europe as
a seat of learning. The core of the old monastery
consists of a roofless cathedral (c900), a well-
preserved Round Tower and St. Kevin's Church,
roofed with stone. Overlooking the Upper Lake,
about a mile away, is another enchanting church
called Reefert. There are good walks in the
surrounding woods. The visitor center also acts as
an information outlet for the Wicklow Mountains
National Park. Being such an important attraction it
can get very busy in high summer.

MALAHIDE CASTLE

Malahide Castle stands in a wooded area, north of Dublin.

Apart from an interlude during the rule of Oliver Cromwell in the mid-17th century, the castle stayed in the hands of the Talbot family from c1200 until 1973. The core of the castle is a medieval tower, and in the adjoining banqueting hall the walls are hung with portraits. Most furnishings are Georgian. Enjoy a tour of the castle rooms, the Avoca gift shop and café (▷ panel, 106), plus the visitors' center in the courtyard. Also visit the walled and botanic gardens, replanted in 2012.

THE BASICS

www.malahidecastleand
gardens.ie
Distance: 13km (8 miles)
Journey Time: 45 min
☎ 846 2184
🕐 Mon–Sat 10–5; Apr–end
Sep Sun 10–5; Oct–end Mar
Sun 11–5
🚌 42
🚆 From Connolly Station
to Malahide, then a 10-min
walk

POWERSCOURT

Beautifully set in the heart of the wild Wicklow Mountains, yet only an hour from Dublin, this house is renowned for its magnificent gardens.

Careful restoration has converted the 18th-century Palladian mansion into an excellent Avoca store (▷ panel, 106) with a terrace café. It is in a dramatic setting, with the cone-shape Sugar Loaf mountain in the distance. To the south, the house looks out over magnificently proportioned stepped terraces, with ornamental sculpture and a statue throwing a jet of water high in the air. Gardens stretch to either side; the one to the east is Japanese, the other walled, with wrought-iron gates. (The story goes that when the terraces' designer, Daniel Robertson, went to inspect the work every morning, he was pushed around in a wheel-barrow, swigging sherry.) You can walk to the waterfall 5km (3 miles) away (additional entrance fee), but it is easier to get there by car.

THE BASICS

www.powerscourt.ie
Distance: 19km (12 miles)
Journey Time: 1 hour
☎ 204 6000
🕐 Daily 9.30–5.30
(gardens close at dusk
in winter)
🚌 44 to Enniskerry, then
walk
🚆 DART to Bray, then 185
feeder bus to Enniskerry
❓ Waterfall inadvisable
on foot

Shopping

BLANCHARDSTOWN CENTRE
www.blanchardstowncentre.ie
One of Ireland's biggest malls, the Blanchardstown Centre is a 20-minute drive northwest of Dublin. It has the best selection of price-wise and fashionable retail names under one roof in the Dublin area, plus cinemas, restaurants, free parking. Many stores open until 9pm Monday to Friday.
Off map ✉ Blanchardstown ☎ 822 1356 🚃 Suburban line Connolly to Blanchardstown 🚌 37, 39, 76A, 220, 236

DUNDRUM TOWN CENTRE
www.dundrum.ie
Just south of central Dublin and only a 22-minute ride on the Luas, this is one of the largest and most modern shopping venues in Ireland. There are more than 120 stores, with big names such as Harvey Nichols and House of Fraser, restaurants, cafés and bars. There is also a 12-screen cinema and a multifunctional arts venue, the Mill Theatre.
Off map ✉ Dundrum 🚌 17, 14A; Luas Sandyford

BLACKROCK MARKET
Bargain hunters flock to Blackrock, 8km (5 miles) south of Dublin, for the market held every Saturday 11–5.30 and Sunday 12–5.30. Also holiday Mondays 11–5.30. Stalls sell clothes, bric-à-brac, fine art, crafts and antiques. There are usually around 50 traders, plus refreshment stands.
Off map ✉ Blackrock ☎ 283 3522; www.blackrockmarket.com ✉ Blackrock 🚌 G7, 7A, 8, 17

LIFFEY VALLEY SHOPPING CENTRE
www.liffeyvalley.ie
A 20-minute drive southwest of Dublin with more than 90 retail outlets, including Tommy Hilfiger and Diesel. The food court has 16 restaurants and cafés, including Eddie Rockets Diner and Harry Ramsden's. There is also a 14-screen cinema.
Off map ✉ Fonthill Road, Clondalkin 🚌 25, 66, 78A

THE SQUARE, TALLAGHT
www.thesquare.ie
The Square in Tallaght, just south of Dublin, has nearly 150 shops under a dome of natural light. It has a UCI cinema, fast-food restaurants, a free crèche, a bowling alley, pubs nearby and parking for some 3,000 cars.
Off map ✉ Tallaght ☎ 452 5944 🚌 50; Luas Tallaght

Entertainment and Nightlife

BLANCHARDSTOWN ODEON
A nine-screen multiplex outside the city. Films tend to run longer here than at the more central cinemas.
Off map ✉ Blanchardstown Shopping Centre ☎ 1520 880000 🚃 Suburban line Connolly to Blanchardstown 🚌 38A, 39A, 39C, 70, 236

CIVIC THEATRE
www.civictheatre.ie
A community arts venue in the southwest suburbs providing contemporary dance, opera and classical music. Art gallery, café and bar.
Off map ✉ Blessington Road, off Belguard Square East, Tallaght ☎ 462 7477 🚌 49, 50, 54A, 65, 77; Luas Tallaght

GAELIC GAMES
www.gaa.ie; www.crokepark.ie
Gaelic football and hurling are fast, physical games, and the All-Ireland finals are played before

sell-out crowds in early and late September. Immensely popular.

⊞ J3 ⊠ Croke Park Stadium, St. Joseph's Avenue ☎ 819 2300 🚌 11, 16, 51A

THE HELIX
www.thehelix.ie
This modern arts complex at the City University has three auditoria—the 1,260-capacity Mahony Hall, the smaller 450-seat Theatre and the 150-seat Space. It serves up a mixed programme of classical concerts, drama and ballet, plus rock and pop music.
⊞ Off map ⊠ Dublin City University, Collins Avenue, Glasnevin ☎ 700 7000 🚌 4, 11, 13, 16, 44

HORSERACING
www.leopardstown.com
Leopardstown Race Course is one of Ireland's busiest. Open all year, it hosts the Hennessy Gold Cup and a traditional post-Christmas festival, among other events.
⊞ Off map
⊠ Leopardstown ☎ 289 0500 🚋 Luas Sandyford

JOHN KAVANAGH
Adjacent to Glasnevin Cemetery, this pub is known by locals as 'The Gravediggers'. Folklore has it that it was where workers would head for a pint after their duties. Little has changed inside since it opened in 1833.
⊞ G1 ⊠ 1 Prospect Square ☎ 830 7978 🚌 13, 19, 40

JOHNNIE FOX'S
www.jfp.ie
People come from near and far for the turf fires, live traditional music, céilí dancing and tasty seafood. If you want to eat, reserve ahead.
⊞ Off map ⊠ Glencullen, ☎ 295 5647 🚌 Special express bus—reservations advisable (☎ 822 1122, www.expressbus.ie)

ROLLERBLADING
The smooth, flat, picturesque walk along Sandymount Strand is popular with local in-line skaters who whoosh along the waterfront day and night. A stunning location in both spring and summer.
⊞ Off map ⊠ Sandymount Strand, Sandymount 🚌 2, 3

RUGBY
Ireland's fans are always enthusiastic when it

GOLF
The growth of championship golf courses in Dublin is staggering—the 2006 Ryder Cup was held at the K Club near Dublin. Many clubs welcome non-members, and fees are reasonable. The most famous are Portmarnock and Royal Dublin; also try Castle, Grange, Woodbrook Malahide, Miltown, Hermitage and Island, or try one of the city's pitch-and-putt courses. The Irish Open Golf Championships are staged in July.

---

comes to their national team. Details of fixtures for local clubs, like Bective Rangers and Wesley, are published in the local press. The Aviva Stadium, built on the site of the old Lansdowne Road Stadium, opened in 2010 and is the home for Ireland's national rugby team. Or you could watch a game in one of the many pubs showing big matches on screen.
⊞ M9 ⊠ Aviva Lansdowne Road Stadium, Ballsbridge ☎ 647 3800 🚉 Lansdowne Road 🚌 5, 7, 7A, 45

SOCCER
Since the World Cup in 1990, the Irish have become soccer fanatics, and Dublin usually stands still when the national team plays. The season runs from March to November. You can buy tickets for Shamrock Rovers' matches (Tallaght Stadium) at the gate.
⊞ Off map ⊠ Tallaght Stadium, Whitestown Way ☎ 460 5948 🚌 49, 65; Luas Tallaght

VUE
www.myvue.ie
Ireland's biggest multiplex cinema has 14 screens. Seats look and feel like sports cars, and sound and picture quality are state-of-the-art, as are the dining facilities.
⊞ Off map ⊠ Liffey Valley Centre, Fonthill Road, Clondalkin ☎ 1520 501000 🚌 78A, 210, 239

FARTHER AFIELD ENTERTAINMENT AND NIGHTLIFE

Restaurants

PRICES

Prices are approximate, based on a 3-course meal for one person.

€€€	over €40
€€	€25–€40
€	under €25

BELLA CUBA (€€)

www.bella-cuba.com

Tasty Cuban dishes served with a smile in a tropical atmosphere accompanied by salsa music.

✚ Off map ✉ 11 Ballsbridge Terrace ☎ 660 5539 🕔 Dinner daily 🚇 Lansdowne Road 🚌 5, 6, 7, 8, 45, 84

CAVISTONS (€€)

www.cavistons.com

Immensely popular gourmet seafood restaurant that arose from the success of the nearby food emporium. Menu changes daily.

✚ Off map ✉ 59 Glasthule Road, Sandycove ☎ 280 9245 🕔 Lunch Tue–Sat, dinner Fri, Sat (6–8pm) 🚇 Sandycove and Glasthule 🚌 59

CHI (€€)

On a quiet street in the suburb of Blackrock, this is a smart, modern Asian restaurant serving great Asian fusion food. The dining room is sleek; the staff smart and attentive. There are tasty Thai curries and a gamut of Asian goodies to try. Set menus or individual dishes are available.

✚ Off map ✉ 9 Georges Avenue, Blackrock ☎ 210 8622 🕔 Lunch Mon–Fri, dinner daily 🚇 Blackrock 🚌 7, 7A, 8, 17

GUINEA PIG (THE FISH RESTAURANT) (€€€)

www.guineapig.dalkey.info

Attractive, family-run restaurant, with an extensive seafood-based and vegetarian menu. In business since 1957, it is one of Ireland's longest established restaurants; and deservedly so. Top food and service.

✚ Off map ✉ 17 Railway Road, Dalkey ☎ 285 9055 🕔 Dinner only 🚇 Dalkey 🚌 59

HARTLEY'S (€€)

www.hartleys.ie

A sophisticated setting for fish, chargrills, pasta and salads. Overlooking the harbor. Mussels and chargrilled steak are signature dishes.

✚ Off map ✉ 1 Harbour Road, Dun Laoghaire ☎ 280 6767 🕔 Lunch and dinner Tue–Sun 🚇 Dun Laoghaire 🚌 7

KING SITRIC (€€€)

www.kingsitric.ie

The fish are landed a few yards from Dublin's most regal seafood restaurant, named after the 11th-centry Norse king of Dublin. It's been going strong for 40 years and is popular with Dublin high society. Chef Patron Aidan presides over a wonderful menu and wine cellar. The more casual East Café Bar, on the same site, is open daily.

✚ Off map ✉ East Pier, Howth ☎ 832 5235 🕔 Summer lunch and dinner Wed–Mon; winter lunch Sun, dinner Thu–Sat 🚇 Howth 🚌 31, 31B

THE LOBSTER POT

www.thelobsterpot.ie

This family-run seafood restaurant has been a huge hit with Ballsbridge locals since 1980. There's an elegant dining room, and a roaring fire in the evenings. Classic signature dishes include Dublin Bay king prawns and fresh lobster Thermidor, plus fine cuts of meat.

✚ Off map ✉ 9 Ballsbridge Terrace ☎ 668 0025 🕔 Dinner Mon–Sat 🚇 Landsdowne Road

AVOCA CAFÉS

The Avoca Handweavers were founded in 1723, and in recent years their award-winning cafés have been talked about as much as their famous shops. You can find branches in the village of Avoca, the home of the original mill, at Kilmacanoge near Bray, at Powerscourt House (▷ 103) and in the middle of Dublin in Suffolk Street. Homemade is the key word and the delicious desserts are especially noteworthy, along with great scones, biscuits and cakes.

From boutique hotels to elegant Georgian town houses, there are some great choices when deciding where to stay in Dublin, but it's expensive. North of the river bed-and-breakfast is a less-expensive option.

Introduction

Dublin has long been considered an expensive place to visit, but the downturn in the Irish and world economies has led to a big drop in prices at the wide range of hotels and guesthouses in the city. There are bargains to be found for your stay here.

Accommodation Options

Exclusive hotels in the heart of the city, in particular around St. Stephen's Green and Merrion Square, offer high standards and prices to match. For good quality and value, try the townhouse hotels or stay in the quieter suburbs such as leafy Ballsbridge (Dublin 4), known as the 'embassy' area. A short bus ride or 15-minute walk into town, it is also convenient for the Aviva Stadium at Lansdowne Road, the O2, Financial Centre and Docklands. Hostels offer the cheapest budget options and often include free breakfast and internet use.

Reservation Advice

A large number of travelers choose to make their reservations on the internet, and it pays to compare prices on several sites, including the website of your chosen hotel, which may have some good-value packages not available through accommodation-only sites. During special events like rugby internationals the city can seem invaded, and hotel rates rise accordingly. Traditionally, prices have always included a full Irish breakfast, but many places are now offering room-only rates, with the full breakfast a separate option. If you have not booked in advance, Dublin Tourism in Suffolk Street offers an on-the-spot booking service, for Dublin and across the whole of Ireland.

SELF-CATERING

Most self-catering options are in the suburbs or at the coast, but there are some in the city. Check out www.visitdublin.com, which is a good place to start your search for whatever style of accommodation you are seeking.

Budget Hotels

ABBERLEY COURT

www.abberley.ie
Next to an excellent complex of shops, restaurants and a cinema, this smart 38-room hotel includes a lounge bar with live entertainment, nightclub and restaurant.
🚇 Off map ✉ Belgard Road, Tallaght ☎ 459 6000 🚌 49, 50, 65, 65B, 75, 77; Luas Tallagh

AVALON HOUSE

www.avalon-house.ie
This purpose-built hostel offers single, double, triple, quad and dormitory rooms, in neat, fresh surroundings. Breakfast, café and free WiFi.
🚇 G8 ✉ 55 Aungier Street ☎ 475 0001 🚌 Cross-city buses

BARNACLES TEMPLE BAR HOUSE

www.barnacles.ie
Highly rated Temple Bar hostel with DVD and games room, self-catering facilities and breakfast room. Dormitory-style rooms and en suite.
🚇 G7 ✉ 19 Temple Lane South ☎ 671 6277 🚉 Tara Street 🚌 Cross-city buses

BEWLEY'S NEWLANDS CROSS

www.bewleyshotels.com
Good amenities and spacious 258 bedrooms, furnished to a high standard. A bit outside the city so best if you have a car.
🚇 Off map ✉ Newland's Cross, Naas Road, Clondalkin ☎ 464 0140 🚌 51, 68

ISAAC'S HOSTEL

www.isaacs.ie
Good value hostel, popular with young backpackers, with a range of private rooms and larger dormitories. Shared lounge area with free WiFi, laundry and simple kitchen.
🚇 J6 ✉ 2–5 Frenchman's Lane ☎ 855 6215 🚌 Cross-city buses; Luas Busáras

KINLAY HOUSE

www.kinlayhouse.ie
A good hostel with 39 rooms to suit different budgets—from dormitory-style to en suite twins. Continental breakfast included. Can be noisy at night. TV lounge.
🚇 G7 ✉ 2–12 Lord Edward Street ☎ 679 6644 🚌 Cross-city buses

MARIAN GUEST HOUSE

www.marianguesthouse.ie
In elegant Georgian Dublin, 5 to 10 minutes' walk from the city's principal attractions. Friendly, family-run, with 17 tasteful rooms.
🚇 H4 ✉ 21 Gardiner Street Upper ☎ 874 4129 🚉 Connolly 🚌 41A

O'SHEAS

www.osheashotel.com
Warm and friendly hotel close to the shopping districts and sights, with 34 attractive rooms, bar, lounge and restaurant.
🚇 H5 ✉ 19 Talbot Street ☎ 836 5670 🚉 Connolly 🚌 Cross-city buses

OLIVER ST. JOHN GOGARTY

www.gogartys.ie
Budget rooms right in the heart of Temple Bar. Be prepared for a lively stay, with the bar and restaurant always packed and plenty of traditional music in the upstairs bar.
🚇 H7 ✉ 18–21 Anglesea Street ☎ 671 1822 🚉 Connolly 🚌 Cross-city buses

TRINITY COLLEGE

www.tcd.ie
If you are planning a long stay in the summer, it is possible to rent student rooms in Trinity College at reasonable rates. Some have their own bathrooms and kitchens.
🚇 H7 ✉ College Green ☎ 896 4477 🚉 Pearse, Tara Street 🚌 Cross-city buses

Mid-Range Hotels

PRICES

Expect to pay between €80 and €150 for a double room in a mid-range hotel

ABERDEEN LODGE

www.aberdeen-lodge.com
Just a short DART ride from central Dublin, this fine Edwardian house with 16 en suite rooms ensures a comfortable and quiet stay in an attractive suburb. Some of the rooms have four-poster beds and all come well equipped.
➕ Off map ✉ 53 Park Avenue, Ballsbridge ☎ 283 8155 🚇 Sydney Parade

ARIEL HOUSE

www.ariel-house.net
A gracious Victorian house in the suburb of Ballsbridge. Good standard in all 37 rooms; tasty breakfasts—with vegetarian options. Friendly staff. Secure parking.
➕ L9 ✉ 50–54 Landsdowne Road, Ballsbridge ☎ 668 5512 🚇 Lansdowne Road 🚌 7, 45

ARLINGTON HOTEL TEMPLE BAR

www.arlingtonhoteltemplebar.com
The Arlington (formerly the Parliament Hotel) is opposite Dublin Castle and just around the corner from Temple Bar. There are 63 well-furnished rooms. Celtic nights are held in the Legends bar.

➕ G7 ✉ Lord Edward Street ☎ 670 8777 🚌 Cross-city buses

BUSWELLS

www.buswells.ie
Comprising five Georgian town houses, Buswells is one of Dublin's oldest hotels and a poular meeting place for MPs from the Dail opposite.
➕ H7 ✉ 23–25 Molesworth Street ☎ 614 6500 🚇 Pearse 🚌 Cross-city buses

CASSIDY'S HOTEL

www.cassidyshotel.com
Family-run, 113-room hotel in a Georgian terrace at the top end of O'Connell Street. Grooms Bar and Bistro are an added bonus. Parking places are limited.
➕ H5 ✉ 6–8 Cavendish Row, O'Connell Street Upper ☎ 878 0555 🚌 Cross-city buses

ALL THE OPTIONS

As you'd expect from a lively, modern and cosmopolitan capital, Dublin offers every type and style of place to stay, from budget hostels and self-catering to good value Georgian town houses converted into charming hotels or guesthouses, trendy boutique hotels and luxury 5-star establishments. Don't be afraid to choose a place in the suburbs. Room rates are lower and Dublin's excellent public transportation system will get you into the heart of the city in a short time.

DEER PARK HOTEL GOLF & SPA

www.deerpark-hotel.ie
Only 14km (8.5 miles) from the heart of the city, on a quiet hillside in the grounds of Howth Castle and overlooking the sea. Large golf complex and spa; 78 rooms.
➕ Off map ✉ Howth ☎ 832 2624 🚇 (DART) Howth

GRAFTON CAPITAL

www.graftoncapitalhotel.com
In the heart of Dublin's shopping and cultural area, with many restaurants, cafés and attractions just around the corner. Traditional Georgian town house with 75 elegant rooms.
➕ G7 ✉ Stephen's Street Lower ☎ 648 1100 🚇 Pearse 🚌 Cross-city buses

GRAND CANAL HOTEL

www.grandcanalhotel.ie
Part of the new canal complex, this purpose-built hotel has 142 rooms and is conveniently situated for the O2 arena and Aviva Stadium.
➕ L8 ✉ 13–27 Upper Grand Canal Street ☎ 646 1000 🚇 Grand Canal Dock 🚌 5, 7, 7A, 8, 18, 27X, 45

HARDING HOTEL

www.hardinghotel.ie
Hardings looks the part with clever interior design and artwork on the walls. It is packed with atmosphere thanks to a lively hotel bar and Copper

Alley Bistro. 52 rooms.
G7 ✉ Copper Alley, Fishamble Street ☎ 679 6500 🚌 Cross-city buses

HARRINGTON HALL

www.harringtonhall.com
A beautifully restored Georgian guesthouse with genteel public areas and 28 generously proportioned guest rooms. An elegant address near St. Stephen's Green.
G9 ✉ 70 Harcourt Street ☎ 475 3497 🚌 Cross-city buses

HERBERT PARK HOTEL

www.herbertparkhotel.ie
If you don't mind being a little out of the city center, then this hotel offers excellent value. Overlooking a leafy park, it has conference and meeting facilities, and slick guest rooms. An easy walk to the Aviva Stadium and the O2.
Off map ✉ Pembroke Place, Ballsbridge ☎ 667 2200 🚉 Landsowne Road

JURYS INN CUSTOM HOUSE

www.jurysinns.com
In the financial district by the redeveloped docks, this Jury's hotel is of a high standard. Some of the rooms are large enough to accommodate two adults and two children comfortably. 239 rooms.
J6 ✉ Custom House Dock ☎ 854 1500 🚉 Connolly 🚊 Luas Busáras

MESPIL

www.mespilhotel.com
Efficient, spacious and modern; 255 rooms, some overlooking the Grand Canal.
J9 ✉ 50–60 Mespil Road ☎ 488 4600 🚉 Grand Canal Dock 🚊 10

MOLESWORTH COURT SUITES

www.molesworthcourt.ie
The one- and two-bedroom apartments (12 in all) can be rented for one night or more. Near Grafton Street.
H8 ✉ Schoolhouse Lane, off Molesworth Street ☎ 676 4799 🚉 Pearse 🚌 Cross-city buses

THE MORGAN

www.themorgan.com
Egyptian cotton sheets,

GOLF HOTELS

Ireland's reputation as a world-class golfing destination is now undisputed; and there are some excellent hotels with great courses just outside the city. Try the Portmarnock Hotel and Golf Links renowned for comfort, good food and world-class golf. The hotel's 18-hole course was designed by Bernard Langer. Conveniently close to the airport.
Off map ✉ Strand Road, Portmarnock ☎ 846 0611; www.portmarnock.com For another golf hotel option see opposite page for the Deer Park Hotel.

---

spacious bathrooms and excellent in-room facilities in this luxurious boutique hotel. Free use of nearby gym and pool.
H6 ✉ 10 Fleet Street, Temple Bar ☎ 643 7000 🚉 Tara Street 🚌 Cross-city buses

PEMBROKE TOWNHOUSE

www.pembroketownhouse.ie
Elegance merges with modern design in this guesthouse, comprising three Georgian town houses. Excellent service. Parking.
L9 ✉ 90 Pembroke Road, Ballsbridge ☎ 660 0277 🚉 Lansdowne Road 🚊 5, 7, 10, 45

STAUNTON'S ON THE GREEN

www.stauntonsonthegreen.ie
Georgian guesthouse with garden and 30 well-equipped rooms. Perfectly placed close to museums and shops.
H8 ✉ 83 St. Stephen's Green ☎ 478 2300 🚉 Pearse 🚌 Cross-city buses

WYNN'S HOTEL

www.wynnshotel.ie
Housed in a listed building, this large hotel is near many of north Dublin's theaters. Elegant, simple guest rooms. Facilities include a fitness room.
H6 ✉ 35–39 Lower Abbey Street ☎ 874 5131 🚌 Cross-city buses; Luas Abbey Street

Luxury Hotels

PRICES

Expect to pay over €150 for a double room in a luxury hotel

CLARENCE
www.theclarence.ie
Chic, modern interior with suede upholstery and stunning floral arrangements. The 50 rooms are small, apart from the fine duplex penthouse. Owned by Bono and U2.

➕ G7 ✉ 6–8 Wellington Quay ☎ 407 0800 🚇 Tara Street 🚌 Cross-city buses

CONRAD DUBLIN
www.hilton.com
Contemporary classic rooms and suites near St. Stephen's Green. Business facilities, baby-sitting services, gym.

➕ H9 ✉ Earlsfort Terrace ☎ 602 8900 🚇 Pearse 🚌 Cross-city buses

THE DAWSON HOTEL & SPA
www.thedawson.ie
Luxury boutique hotel (formerly La Stampa Hotel) with 28 individually designed rooms and suites. The spa provides holistic therapies.

➕ H8 ✉ 35 Dawson Street ☎ 677 4444 🚌 Cross-city buses

DYLAN
www.dylan.ie
Boutique hotel with 44 glamorous rooms and suites. First-rate facilities and plenty of style. Smart restaurant, buzzy bar.

➕ K9 ✉ Eastmoreland Place ☎ 660 3000 🚌 10

FITZWILLIAM
www.fitzwilliamhoteldublin.com
Contemporary style and Irish warmth in a central location. Some of the 130 bedrooms overlook an internal rooftop garden.

➕ H8 ✉ St. Stephen's Green ☎ 478 7000 🚇 Pearse 🚌 Cross-city buses

GRESHAM
www.gresham-hotels.com
The 288 huge, elegant bedrooms combine traditional style with modern comfort. Several bars and lounges, the Gallery restaurant and use of a gym.

THE SHELBOURNE

The illustrious Shelbourne Hotel, built in 1824, has been splendidly restored, retaining its original features while maintaining facilities in the 265 spacious luxurious rooms to the highest modern standard. It has hosted the royal and famous throughout its history. If you can't afford to stay here, why not drop in for afternoon tea. Also excellent food in the Saddle Room and Oyster Bar (▷ 88).

➕ H8 ✉ 27 St. Stephen's Green ☎ 663 4500; www.marriott.co.uk 🚇 Pearse 🚌 Cross-city buses

➕ H5 ✉ 23 O'Connell Street Upper ☎ 874 6881 🚇 Connolly 🚌 Cross-city buses

HERBERT PARK
www.herbertparkhotel.ie
Modern, bright, airy hotel in Dublin's exclusive residential area. Quiet comfort, with 153 rooms overlooking the peaceful Herbert Park.

➕ Off map ✉ Herbert Park, Ballsbridge ☎ 667 2200 🚇 Lansdowne Road 🚌 7, 45

MERRION
www.merrionhotel.com
This impressively restored hotel, originally four Georgian houses, has 140 luxurious bedrooms. Gym, pool, spa and business facilities.

➕ J8 ✉ Merrion Street Upper ☎ 603 0600 🚇 Pearse 🚌 Cross-city buses

THE MORRISON
www.morrisonhotel.ie
Modern designer heaven welcoming a celebrity clientele, with 138 rooms, suites and studios, plus lobby bars and restaurants. Stunning penthouse.

➕ G6 ✉ Ormond Quay Lower ☎ 887 4200 🚌 Cross-city buses

WESTBURY
www.doylecollection.com
Indulge yourself at this stylish hotel with 205 rooms in Dublin's premier shopping street.

➕ H7 ✉ Grafton Street ☎ 679 1122 🚇 Pearse 🚌 Cross-city buses

Dublin is compact and easy to get around on foot. However, buses are numerous and frequent, and the DART is great to use for a trip outside the city. Dublin is a fairly safe city, but keep alert against petty crime.

Planning Ahead

When to Go

Most visitors come between March and October, when the weather is at its best and there is a wider choice of activities. A few attractions are closed in the winter. Dublin is temperate year-round but rain is frequent.

TIME

Ireland is five hours ahead of New York, eight hours ahead of Los Angeles and the same as London.

AVERAGE DAILY MAXIMUM TEMPERATURES

JAN	FEB	MAR	APR	MAY	JUN	JUL	AUG	SEP	OCT	NOV	DEC
46°F	46°F	50°F	55°F	59°F	64°F	68°F	66°F	63°F	57°F	50°F	46°F
8°C	8°C	10°C	13°C	15°C	18°C	20°C	19°C	17°C	14°C	10°C	8°C

Spring (March to May) is mild with mostly clear skies and a mix of sunshine and showers. April and May are the driest months.

Summer (June to August) is bright and warm but notoriously unpredictable. July is particularly showery. Heat-waves are rare.

Autumn (September to November) often has very heavy rain and is mostly overcast, although still quite mild. Even October can be summery.

Winter (December to February) is not usually severe and tends to be wet rather than snowy. Temperatures rarely fall below freezing.

WHAT'S ON

January Temple Bar Tradfest.

February Jameson Dublin International Film Festival.

February/March Six Nations Rugby at the Aviva Stadium.

March St. Patrick's Day Festival (several days around St. Patrick's Day, 17 Mar).

12 Points Festival of Europe's New Jazz.

April Dublin Opera Spring season.

May Dublin Writers Fesival.

April–May International Dance Festival.

June Women's Mini Marathon.

Bloomsday (around 16 Jun): celebration of hero of James Joyce's novel Ulysses.

Docklands Maritime Festival (Bank Hol weekend).

Pride: week-long gay festival.

June–August Music in parks.

July Dublin Circus Festival in Temple Bar.

July–August Jameson Movies on the Square in Temple Bar.

Late August/early September Liffey Swim.

All-Ireland Hurling and Gaelic Football Finals at Croke Park.

September/October Dublin Theatre Festival.

October Adidas Dublin City Marathon.

Samhain Festival: parade and fireworks (31 Oct).

November/December Dublin Opera Winter Season.

December National Crafts Fair.

Christmas Carols, concerts: in churches around the city.

Listings

Daily newspapers cover what's on in Dublin. Pick up a copy of Dublin in Your Pocket and look for The Event Guide, free from clubs, cafés and restaurants around the city.

Useful Websites

www.visitdublin.com
The local tourist board site unveils every aspect of the city via its efficient search engine. You'll find up-to-date information on accommodation (reserve online), restaurants, shopping, nightlife and attractions, as well as insider guides and downloadable city walking tours.

www.templebar.ie
Look here for what's on now, forthcoming events and venues throughout Dublin's Cultural Quarter.

www.irishtimes.com
Influential website of the *Irish Times*, one of Dublin's daily newspapers. Gen up on the news, weather and what's on.

www.irish-architecture.com
The Dublin section under Buildings of Ireland is particularly useful (via 'Leinster').

www.dublinevents.com
A comprehensive guide about forthcoming events at venues across Dublin, from theater and cinema to live music, comedy, concerts, exhibitions and sports. Plus hotels, restaurants, clubbing et al.

www.dublin-culture.com
Another all-encompassing website spanning travel, attractions, entertainment and sport in the city.

www.heritageireland.ie
Useful in-depth information about historical sites and gardens throughout Ireland.

www.ireland.com
Tourism Ireland's site carries a wealth of information on the whole of Ireland, with sections on history, culture, events, activities, accommodation and gastronomy, plus plenty of practical tips.

PRIME TRAVEL SITES

www.fodors.com
A complete travel-planning site. You can research prices and weather; book air tickets, cars and rooms; ask questions (and get answers) from fellow travelers; and find links to other sites.

www.dublinbus.ie
Everything you could possibly need to know about the public bus service, including how to buy the best tickets for your needs. Also information about the DART system and the Luas trams.

INTERNET CAFÉS

Global Internet Café
All you need digitally plus left luggage service and low cost phone calls. Fairtrade and organic coffees and teas served.
✚ H6 ✉ 8 Lower O'Connell Street ☎ 878 0295 🕐 Mon–Fri 8–11, Sat 9–11, Sun 10–11 💷 Varies according to time of day

@ Viva Internet Café
The usual essentials plus computer repair. Near Dublin Castle.
✚ G7 ✉ Unit 1, Lord Edward Street ☎ 672 4725 🕐 Mon–Fri 10am–11pm, Sat–Sun 10.30–10 💷 Varies according to time of day

NEED TO KNOW PLANNING AHEAD

Getting There

ENTRY REQUIREMENTS

Ireland is a member of the European Union. For the latest passport and visa information visit the Embassy of Ireland Great Britain website www.embassyofireland.co.uk or Embassy of Ireland USA www.embassyofireland.org.

CUSTOMS

The limits for non-EU visitors are 200 cigarettes or 50 cigars, or 250g of tobacco; 1 liter of spirits (over 22 percent) or 2 liters of fortified wine, 4 liters of still wine; 50g of perfume. Visitors under 18 are not entitled to the tobacco and alcohol allowances. The guidelines for EU residents (for personal use) are 800 cigarettes, 200 cigars, 1kg tobacco; 10 liters of spirits (over 22 per cent), 20 liters of aperitifs, 90 litres of wine, of which 60 can be sparkling wine, 110 liters of beer.

AIRPORTS

Dublin Airport (www.dublinairport.com) is 11km (7 miles) north of the city. It is the eighth busiest airport in Europe for international passenger traffic, serving more than 160 routes with around 55 airlines to the UK and continental Europe, USA, Canada, North Africa and the Middle East.

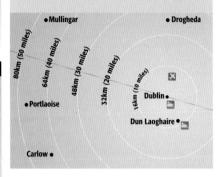

ARRIVING BY AIR

For information on Dublin Airport ☎ 814 1111. Airlink 747 run between the airport and the main city rail and bus stations. The journey takes 20–30 minutes and costs €6. Aircoach is a 24-hour luxury coach service serving central Dublin and the main hotels in Ballsbridge/ Donnybrook and Leopardstown/ Sandyford. The fare ranges from €6 to €9. It also has services to Belfast and Cork. Taxis are metered, and a journey to central Dublin should cost around €30 (but check first). Car rental companies have desks in the arrivals area.

ARRIVING BY BOAT

Ferries from Holyhead sail into the ports of Dublin and Dun Laoghaire throughout the year. The journey takes around 3 hours 15 minutes on a traditional ferry or 2 hours 20 minutes via the high-speed options. Taxis and buses operate from both ports into the city. The DART light train is easily accessible from Dun Laoghaire, which is 14km (9 miles) from the city hub. When traveling by car from Dun Laoghaire port, take the N31 to Blackrock. Turn left onto Mount

Merrion Avenue and continue to N11. Turn right and head north to get into town. From Dublin Port take Alexander Road west, turn left at the O2 and follow 'city centre' signs.

ARRIVING BY TRAIN
There are two main line stations in Dublin. Passengers from the north of Ireland arrive at Connolly Station, while trains from the south and west operate in and out of Heuston Station. Buses and taxis are available at both stations. Irish Rail is at ☎ 1850 366 222; www.irishrail.ie.

ARRIVING BY CAR
Traffic drives on the left. Congestion in Dublin is notorious, and on-street parking is expensive and limited. There are multistory car parks in the city hub. The one-way traffic systems can be confusing. Avoid rush hours, keep out of bus lanes and use designated parking areas. Penalties for illegal parking are severe. Check whether your hotel or guesthouse has parking for guests. Always lock your car and keep belongings out of sight.

INSURANCE
Check your insuance coverage and buy a supplementary policy if needed. EU nationals receive reduced-cost medical treatment with an EHIC card. Obtain this card before leaving home. Full health and travel insurance is still advised.

EMBASSIES IN DUBLIN
● Australia
www.ireland.embassy.gov.au
● Belgium www.diplomatie. be/dublin
● France www.ambafrance-ie.org
● Germany
www.dublin.diplo.de
● Netherlands
www.netherlandsembassy.ie
● United Kingdom www. britishembassyinireland.fco. gov.uk
● United States
www.dublin.usembassy.gov

For addresses and telephone of the above embassies and consulates, and for information on other countries
▷ 122.

Getting Around

TAXIS
● Useful numbers:
NCR Taxis
☎ 677 2222; www.ncr.ie
Blue Cabs
☎ 802 2222;
www.bluecabs.ie.
See local telephone books for others or ask your hotel to call you a cab.

PUBLIC TRANSPORTATION

The bus number and destination (in English and Irish) are displayed on the front. *An Lar* means city center. Buy tickets on the bus (exact change needed) or before boarding from Dublin Bus office or some newsstands; timetables are also available here. Busáras, the main bus terminus, is north of the River Liffey on Amiens Street.

The DART is a light rail service running from Malahide or Howth in the north of the city to Greystones in the south. The main city stations are Connolly (north side) and Pearse (south side). Trains run at least every 5 minutes at peak times, otherwise every 15 minutes Mon–Sat 6.30am–11.30pm and less frequently Sun, 9.30am–11pm. Buy tickets at the station. The Luas is a tram system operating between the suburbs and central Dublin (www.luas.ie). Taxis are in short supply, especially at night. Taxi stands are found outside hotels, train and bus stations, and at locations such as St. Stephen's Green and O'Connell Street.

● Dublin Bus (Bus Átha Cliath) operates Mon–Sat 5am–11.30pm, Sun 8am–11.30pm. Check for individual routes (☎ 873 4222; www.dublinbus.ie).
● Nitelink operates Fri–Sat to the suburbs. Buses leave on the hour from D'Olier Street and Westmoreland Street from around midnight to 4.30am; check for individual routes.
● Bus Éireann Expressway operates a nationwide coach service between Dublin and other cities in Ireland (☎ 836 6111; www.buseireann.ie).

TRAVEL PASSES
● The Leap Card, an electronic top-up card for Dublin buses, can be bought for a €5 returnable deposit, topped up with credit. They are not valid for Nitelink, Airlink, ferry services or tours.
● You can buy all travel passes from Dublin Bus ✉ 55 Upper O'Connell Street. Selected newsstands sell a limited number of passes.

Essential Facts

ELECTRICITY
● 220V AC. Most hotels have 110V shaver outlets.
● Plugs have three square pins.

EMERGENCY PHONE NUMBERS
● Police (*garda*), fire and ambulance ☎ 999 (free of charge).

ETIQUETTE
● Dubliners are very friendly, so do not be perturbed if strangers strike up a conversation.
● Do not expect Dubliners to be very punctual. If you are invited to someone's home for dinner, aim to arrive about 10 minutes late.
● Groups of friends and acquaintances usually buy drinks in rounds and if you join them, you will be expected to participate.

GAY AND LESBIAN TRAVELERS
● *The Out Most*, a free monthly newspaper, is available from clubs, bars and bookshops (www.outmost.com).
● Gay and lesbian events in Dublin include the *International Dublin Gay Theater Festival* (May), *Pride* (late June) and the *Lesbian and Gay Film Festival* (late July/August).
● For information and advice, contact: Gay Switchboard Dublin ☎ 872 1055; www.gayswitchboard.ie 🕐 Mon–Fri 6.30pm–9pm, at 2–6, Sun 4–6.

TOURIST INFORMATION
✉ Dublin Airport
✉ Suffolk Street
✉ 14 Upper O'Connell Street
✉ Dun Laoghaire County Hall, Marine Road
All tourist offices are walk-in only. For information phone ☎ 605 7700 (in Ireland) ☎ 0800 703 3028 (UK) or go to www.visitdublin.com

OPENING HOURS
Museums and sights: Most open seven days a week, but some close on Monday, with shorter hours on Sunday. Call for details.
Shops: Open six days a week, some seven days; late-night shopping on Thursday. Supermarkets are open longer hours Wed–Fri. Large suburban shopping malls open Sunday 12–6.
Banks: Mon, Tue, Fri 10–4, Wed 10.30–4, Thu 10–5.

PLACES OF WORSHIP

Ireland is predominantly Catholic; most religious groups have places of worship in Dublin.

Buddhist	Dublin Buddhist Centre ✉ Liberty Corner, 5 James Joyce Street ☎ 817 8933
Church of Ireland	Christ Church Cathedral ✉ Christchurch Place ☎ 677 8099 St. Patrick's Cathedral ✉ St. Patrick's Close ☎ 453 9472
Jewish	Hebrew Congregation ✉ 32A Rathfarnam Road ☎ 492 3751
Methodist	✉ 9c Lower Abbey Street ☎ 874 4668
Muslim	Islamic Cultural Centre of Ireland ✉ 19 Roebuck Road, Clonskeagh ☎ 208 0000
Roman Catholic	St. Mary's Pro Cathedral ✉ Marlborough Street ☎ 475 9674 University Church ✉ 87a St. Stephen's Green ☎ 478 0616

Outhouse Gay Community and Resource Centre ✉ 105 Capel Street ☎ 873 4999; www.outhouse.ie.

MEDICINES AND MEDICAL TREATMENT

● Ambulance ☎ 999 or 112.

● Hospital with 24-hour emergency service: St. Vincent's ✉ Elm Park, Dublin 4 ☎ 221 4000

● Daytime (Mon–Sat) dental facilities: Anne's Lane Dental Clinic ✉ 2 St. Anne's Terrace, Northbrook Lane ☎ 671 8581. For dental referrals: Irish Dental Association ✉ Leopardstown Office Park, Sandyford, Dublin 18 ☎ 295 0072

● Minor ailments can usually be treated at pharmacies, but only a limited range of medication can be dispensed without a prescription.

● Pharmacies open until 10pm: Hickey's Pharmacy ✉ 55 Lower O'Connell Street ☎ 873 0427; City Pharmacy ✉ 14 Dame Street ☎ 670 4523

MONEY MATTERS

● Banks may offer better exchange rates than shops, hotels and bureaux de change.

● The bank at Dublin airport has longer opening hours but charges above-average commission.

● Credit cards and debit cards can be used in most hotels, shops and restaurants and to withdraw cash from ATMs.

● Most large shops, hotels and restaurants accept traveler's checks accompanied by some form of identification.

● Currency cards, which you top-up online, can be used to withdraw cash or as a debit card, with little or no commission.

NEWSPAPERS AND MAGAZINES

● The daily broadsheets, the *Irish Times* and the *Irish Independent*, are printed in Dublin. The local *Evening Herald* is on sale Mon–Fri at midday. The major UK tabloids also produce separate Irish editions.

● International magazines and newspapers are sold in: Eason ✉ 40–42 Lower O'Connell Street and Reads ✉ 24 Nassau Street.
● For events and entertainment listings, check out *Dublin in Your Pocket* and the free *In Dublin*.
● *Hot Press* is Ireland's music magazine and *Image* is Ireland's best-selling women's magazine. UK magazines are widely available.

POST OFFICES
● The GPO in O'Connell Street (☎ 705 7000) is open Mon–Sat 8.30–6. Other post offices are generally open Mon–Fri 9–5.30, and certain city branches also open on Saturday. Some suburban offices still close for an hour at lunchtime.
● Stamps are sold at post offices, some news-stands, hotels and shops. Books of stamps are available from coin-operated machines outside some post offices.
● Postboxes are green.

SENSIBLE PRECAUTIONS
● Dublin is generally safe but be cautious.
● As in all cities around the world, be aware of pickpockets and keep valuables out of sight.
● Watch handbags and wallets in restaurants, hotels, cafés, shops and cinemas. Don't leave handbags on the backs of chairs.
● Make a separate note of all passport, ticket, traveler's checks and credit card numbers.
● Avoid Phoenix Park at night. Women should particularly be cautious around Fitzwilliam and Merrion squares, and adjoining streets after dark. They are prime prostitution areas.
● After dark, women should sit downstairs on buses, or in a busy car on trains. Take a taxi rather than a late-night bus out to the suburbs.

TELEPHONES
● Public telephones use coins or phone cards (sold in post offices and news dealers).
● Operator ☎ 10; directory enquiries ☎ 11850, 11890, 11811

ORGANIZED SIGHTSEEING
● Dublin Bus Tours offer a hop-on, hop-off sightseeing tour. Buy tickets on board or at Dublin Tourism in Suffolk Street.
● The Dublin Literary Pub Crawl visits pubs frequented by literary giants, complete with readings. The tour starts from the Duke pub, Duke Street (☎ 670 5602 🕐 Apr–Oct nightly 7.30pm; Nov–Mar Thu–Sun 7.30pm).
● The Musical Pub Crawl starts from the Oliver St. John Gogarty pub (☎ 475 3313 🕐 Nightly 7.30).
● Take a sightseeing cruise with Liffey River Cruises and learn about life in Dublin from the Vikings to the latest dockside redevelopment (☎ 473 4082 🕐 Mar–Nov daily, sailings from 10.30am).

NATIONAL HOLIDAYS
● 1 January, 17 March, Easter Monday, first Monday in May, June and August, last Monday in October, 25 and 26 December.
● Many businesses close on Good Friday.

TOILETS
● Dublin is not noted for its public toilets: use the facilities at a pub or large store.
● Signs may be in Irish: *mná*: women, *fir*: men.

LOST PROPERTY

Report loss or theft of a passport to the police immediately. Your embassy or consulate can provide further assistance.

Airport ☎ 814 5555
Ferryport ☎ 607 5519
Train ☎ 703 3299 (Heuston), 703 2358 (Connolly)
Dublin Bus ☎ 703 1321
Bus Éireann ☎ 836 6111

STUDENTS

● Dublin is very student-friendly.
● An International Student Identity Card secures discounts in many cinemas, theaters, shops, restaurants and attractions.
● Discounts may be available on travel cards for the bus and DART.

● Avoid calling from hotels where charges are high. Look for public phones on streets, in pubs and shopping malls.
● If you are in Dublin for a longer stay, it could be worthwhile buying a local SIM card for your mobile phone.
● When calling Ireland from the UK dial 00 353. The code for Dublin is 01 (omit the zero when calling from abroad).
● To call the UK from Dublin, dial 00 44.
● When calling from the US dial 011 353. The code for Dublin is 01 (omit the zero when calling from abroad).
● To call the US from Dublin, dial 00 1.

TELEVISION AND RADIO

● Radio Telefis Éireann (RTÉ) is the state broadcasting authority. It has four FM radio stations and five digital radio stations. Its television stations are RTÉ 1, RTÉ 2 and RTÉ News Now.
● TG4 is the National Irish Language station. TV3 Ireland is independent.

EMBASSIES

Australia	✉ Fitzwilton House, Wilton Terrace, Dublin 2 ☎ 664 5300
Belgium	✉ Shrewsbury Road, Dublin 4 ☎ 205 7100
Canada	✉ 7–8 Wilton Terrace, Dublin 2 ☎ 234 4000
France	✉ 36 Ailesbury Road, Dublin 4 ☎ 277 5000
Germany	✉ 31 Trimleston Avenue, Booterstown, County Dublin ☎ 269 3011
Italy	✉ 63 Northumberland Road, Dublin 4 ☎ 660 1744
Netherlands	✉ 160 Merrion Road, Dublin 4 ☎ 269 3444
Spain	✉ 17a Merlyn Park, Sandymount, Dublin 4 ☎ 283 9900
United Kingdom	✉ 29 Merrion Road, Dublin 4 ☎ 205 3700
US	✉ 42 Elgin Road, Ballsbridge, Dublin 4 ☎ 668 8777

Language

Irish is the official first language of the Republic of Ireland with English as the second. Although the Irish language is still alive and studied by all school children, English is the spoken language in Dublin. Irish is rarely spoken, but the language is enjoying a revival and is fashionable among a younger set proud of their cultural traditions. It is an important symbol of national identity. You will come across Irish on signposts, buses, trains and official documents, and the news (*an nuacht*) is broadcast *as gaeilge* on television and radio. Telefís Na Gaeilge's *TG4* is a dedicated Irish-language channel with English subtitles. The areas known as the Gaeltacht are pockets of the country where Irish is the main tongue and you will find maps and signposts only using the Gaelic. These areas are mainly on the western side of Ireland and not in the Dublin vicinity, where English is widely used. The Irish language is difficult for the beginner to grasp, with words often pronounced quite differently to the way they are written. To complicate things further, there are different Irish dialects and spellings in different regions.

SOME IRISH WORDS TO LOOK OUT FOR:

An Lar	City Centre
Baile Átha Cliath	Dublin
Céilí	Dance
Craic	Fun; laughter; good time
Dia dhuit	Hello
Dúnta	Closed
Fáilte	Welcome
Gardaí	Police
Go raibh maith aguth	Thank you
Leitris	Toilet
Mná	Ladies
Fir	Gents
Le do thoil	Please
Níl/ní hea	No
Oifig an phoist	Post Office
Oscailte	Open
Slán	Goodbye
Sláinte	Cheers
Tá/sea	Yes

Timeline

The Celts landed in Ireland in the 4th century BC and their influence remains even today. Their religious rites included complex burial services. Archaeological excavations have produced some magnificent gold pieces and jewelry, some of which can be seen in Dublin's National Museum (▷ 66).

According to legend St. Patrick converted many of Dublin's inhabitants to Christianity in the 5th century AD. In AD841 Vikings established a trading station, probably near present-day Kilmainham. The Vikings moved downstream, to the area around Dublin Castle, in the 10th century.

1014 High King Brian Boru defeats the Dublin Vikings.

1172 After Norman barons invade Ireland from Wales, King Henry II gives Dublin to the men of Bristol.

1348–51 The Black Death claims one third of Dublin's inhabitants.

1592 Queen Elizabeth I grants a charter for the founding of Trinity College.

1700s Dublin's population expands from 40,000 to 172,000.

1712 Work starts on Trinity College Library.

1713 Jonathan Swift is appointed Dean of St. Patrick's Cathedral.

1714 Start of the Georgian era, Dublin's great period of classical architecture.

1745 The building of Leinster House (now home of the Irish Parliament) leads to new housing south of the river.

1759 The Guinness Brewery is founded.

1760–1800 Dublin reaches the height of its prosperity.

1782 The Irish Parliament secures legislative independence from Britain.

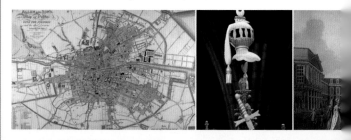

1800 The Act of Union is passed and the Irish Parliament abolishes itself, prefacing a period of urban decline.

1847 Soup kitchens are set up around Dublin during the Great Famine.

1916 The Easter Rising.

1919 First session of Dáil Éireann (the Irish Parliament) in Mansion House.

1922 Civil War declared. After 718 years in residence, British forces evacuate Dublin Castle.

1963 Visit by President John F. Kennedy.

1979 The Pope says mass in Phoenix Park to more than 1.3 million people.

1998 The Good Friday Agreement sees a ceasefire in Northern Ireland.

2001 IRA decommissioned in December.

2007–09 Docklands development continues to thrive with extensions of the Luas and the building of the Samuel Beckett Bridge.

2010 Dublin is European Capital of Sport.

2013 The IMF warns Ireland that its national debt is becoming unsustainable.
Legislation is passed allowing abortion in certain circumstances.

EASTER RISING

With the founding of the Gaelic League in 1893 and the Abbey Theatre in 1904, the movement for independence gathered momentum in Ireland. Frustrated republicans capitalized on England's preoccupation with World War I to stage a rising in 1916 and declare an independent Republic in Dublin's General Post Office. It was doomed to failure but the execution of several of the insurrection's leaders made rebels out of many Irish royalists, leading five years later to the creation of an Irish Free State. The Anglo-Irish Treaty was signed in 1921, followed by a Civil War in 1922, lasting 22 months. In 1936 the Free State became known as Eire under a new Constitution. The Republic finally became a reality in 1949.

From far left: An early city map; helmets in St. Patrick's Cathedral; Great Courtyard of Dublin Castle; Queen Victoria in Dublin at the end of the 19th century

Index

Published by AA Publishing, a trading name of AA Media Limited, whose registered office is Fanum House, Basing View, Basingstoke, Hampshire RG21 4EA. Registered number 06112600.

© **AA Media Limited 2015**
First published 1999
New edition 2015

WRITTEN BY Dr. Peter Harbison and Melanie Morris
ADDITIONAL WRITING Hilary Weston and Jackie Staddon
UPDATED BY Emma Levine
SERIES EDITOR Clare Ashton
COVER DESIGN Tracey Freestone, Nick Johnston
DESIGN WORK Tracey Freestone
IMAGE RETOUCHING AND REPRO Ian Little

Colour separation by AA Digital Department
Printed and bound by Leo Paper Products, China

A CIP catalogue record for this book is available from the British Library.

ISBN 978-0-7495-7658-5

We have tried to ensure accuracy in this guide, but things do change, so please let us know if you have any comments at travelguides@theAA.com.

A05237
Maps in this title based on Ordnance Survey Ireland.
Permit No. 8944
© Ordnance Survey Ireland and Government of Ireland
Transport map © Communicarta Ltd, UK

The Automobile Association would like to thank the following photographers, companies and picture libraries for their assistance in the preparation of this book.

Abbreviations for the picture credits are as follows – (t) top; (b) bottom; (c) centre; (l) left; (r) right; (AA) AA World Travel Library.

1 AA/C Coe; 2 AA/S Day; 3 AA/S Day; 4t AA/S Day; 4l AA/S Whitehorne; 5t AA/S Day; 5c AA/S Whitehorne; 6t AA/S Day; 6cl AA/C Coe; 6c AA/Slidefile; 6cr AA/M Short; 6bl AA/S Day; 6bc AA/S Whitehorne; 6br AA/S McBride; 7t AA/S Day; 7cl AA/L Blake; 7cr AA/S Day; 7bl AA/S Day; 7br AA/S McBride; 8t AA/S Day; 9t AA/S Day; 10t AA/S Day; 10ctr AA/S Whitehorne; 10cr AA/S Day; 10cbr AA/S Whitehorne; 11t AA/S Day; 11ctl AA/S Day; 11cl AA/S Whitehorne; 11cbl AA/S Whitehorne; 12 AA/S Day; 13t AA/S Day; 13ctl AA/Slidefile; 13cl AA/C Coe; 13cbl AA/Slidefile; 13bl AA/C Coe; 14t AA/S Day; 14ctr AA/S McBride; 14cr AA/S Day; 14cbr AA/S Whitehorne; 14br AA/S Whitehorne; 15 AA/S Day; 16t AA/S Day; 16tr AA/S Whitehorne; 16cr Photodisc; 16br AA/D Henley; 17t AA/S Day; 17tl AA/M Short; 17ctl Photodisc; 17cbl AA/M Short; 17bl AA/M Short; 18t AA/S Day; 18tr AA/S Day; 18ctr AA/M Short; 18cbr AA/Slidefile; 18br AA/S Day; 19t Courtesy of Guiness Storehouse; 19ct AA/S Day; 19cb AA/S Day; 19b AA/S Whitehorne; 20/21 AA/S Day; 24l AA/S Day; 24c AA/S Day; 24r AA/S Day; 25l AA/S Whitehorne; 25r AA/Slidefile; 26l AA/S Day; 26c AA/S Day; 26r AA/S Day; 27l Courtesy of Dublinia; 27r Courtesy of Dublinia; 28l AA/S Day; 28r AA/S Day; 28/29 AA/Slidefile; 29t AA/S Day; 29c AA/S Day; 29cr AA/S Day; 30 Courtesy of Guiness Storehouse; 30/31 Courtesy of Guiness Storehouse; 32l AA/S Whitehorne; 32c AA/S Day; 32r AA/S Day; 33l AA/S Day; 33c AA/Slidefile; 33r AA/M Short; 34l AA/S Day; 34r AA/C Coe; 35t AA/Slidefile; 35bl AA/S Day; 35br AA/S Whitehorne; 36 AA/S Whitehorne; 37t AA/S Whitehorne; 38t AA/M Short; 39 AA/S Day; 40t AA/T King; 41t AA/Slidefile; 42t AA/S Day; 43t AA/S Whitehorne; 44t ImageState; 45 Hon Lau - Dublin/Alamy; 48 AA/S Day; 49l Courtesy of Hugh Lane Gallery; 49r AA/Slidefile; 50l AA/S Day; 50c AA/M Short; 50r AA/S Day; 51l AA/S Day; 51cl AA/S Day; 51cr AA/S Day; 51r AA/S Day; 52 AA/S Whitehorne; 52/53 AA/ W Vosey; 54t AA/Slidefile; 54bl AA/Slidefile; 54br AA/Slidefile; 55t AA/Slidefile; 55bl AA/S Whitehorne; 55br AA/S Day; 56t AA/S Whitehorne; 57t AA/S Day; 58t AA/C Coe; 59 AA/M Short; 60t DigitalVision; 60c AA/S McBride; 61 AA/S McBride; 64l AA/ T King; 64r AA/S Day; 65l AA/Slidefile; 65c AA/W Vosey; 65r AA/S Whitehorne; 66 AA/ S Whitehorne; 66/67 AA/S Day; 68l AA/W Vosey; 68r AA/M Short; 69l AA/S Whitehorne; 69r AA/S Whitehorne; 70tl AA/S Whitehorne; 70cl AA/S Day; 70r AA/S Whitehorne; 71t AA/S Day; 71cr AA/S Day; 72t AA/S McBride; 72cl AA/S Day; 72c AA/S Day; 72/73 AA/S McBride; 74t AA/Slidefile; 74bl AA/M Short; 74br Peter Forsberg/Europe/Alamy; 75t AA/Slidefile; 75bl AA/S Whitehorne; 75br AA/Slidefile; 76t AA/Slidefile; 76bl AA/ S Day; 76br AA/S Day; 77 AA/S Whitehorne; 78t AA/S Whitehorne; 79t AA/S Day; 80t AA/M Short; 81t AA/S Whitehorne; 82t AA/M Short; 83t AA/C Coe; 84 Barry Mason/ Alamy; 85t AA/S Day; 86t AA/S Day; 87t ImageState; 88t AA/S Day; 89 AA/C Jones; 92l AA/S Whitehorne; 92r AA/S Whitehorne; 93l AA/S Day; 93r AA/S Day; 94t AA/ S McBride; 94c AA/S Whitehorne; 94/95 AA/S Whitehorne; 96l Courtesy of Irish Museum of Modern Art; 96c Courtesy of Irish Museum of Modern Art; 96r Courtesy of Irish Museum of Modern Art; 97t AA/Slidefile; 97bl AA/S Whitehorne; 97br AA/S Whitehorne; 98t AA/Slidefile; 98b AA/S Whitehorne; 99 AA/M Short; 100t AA/M Short; 100cl AA/ M Short; 100cr AA/M Short; 100br AA/C Jones; 101t AA/M Short; 101bl AA/S Whitehorne; 100br AA/Slidefile; 102t AA/C Jones; 102bl AA/C Jones; 102br AA/ C Jones; 103t AA/C Jones; 103bl AA/Slidefile; 103bc AA/M Short; 103br AA/M Short; 104t AA/M Short; 104c AA/Slidefile; 105t AA/S McBride; 106t ImageState; 107 AA/ C Sawyer; 108t AA/C Sawyer; 108ctr AA/W Vosey; 108cr AA/C Sawyer; 108cbr AA/ M Short; 108br AA/S McBride; 109t AA/C Sawyer; 110t AA/C Sawyer; 111t AA/C Sawyer; 112t AA/C Sawyer; 113 AA/S Day; 114 AA/M Short; 115 AA/M Short; 116 AA/M Short; 117t AA/M Short; 117c AA/C Jones; 117b AA/M Short; 118 AA/ M Short; 119 AA/M Short; 120 AA/M Short; 121t AA/M Short; 122t AA/M Short; 122l AA/C Jones; 123t AA/M Short; 123b AA/S Day; 124t AA/M Short; 124bl AA/ Slidefile; 124bc AA/S Day; 124/125 AA/Slidefile; 125t AA/M Short; 125br AA.

Every effort has been made to trace the copyright holders, and we apologise in advance for any accidental errors. We would be happy to apply the corrections in the following edition of this publication.

Titles in the Series